A Crown of Roses

54-Day Rosary Novena

I dedicate all my work to our Blessed Mother.

This book is the property of Our Lady.
It is for personal use only.
No copies are permitted without my consent.
No distribution is allowed for personal profit.
To be added to the email list or to receive more copies of this book, please contact me at: acrownofrosesnovena@gmail.com
A Crown of Roses
Copyright © 2024 by Barbara Morand
All rights reserved.
First Edition
ISBN: 979-8-9919731-1-3

Forward

What is the Rosary?

According to tradition, Mary appeared to St. Dominic in 1221 and gave him the rosary as a devotional prayer. Similar to monks who prayed all 150 Psalms each day, using beads to track their progress, so the prayers of the rosary are prayed with a set of beads. Many reported apparitions of Mary, including those of Lourdes and Fatima in more recent times, as well as those in history, involve her invocation to pray the rosary for the world.

To pray the rosary, you follow a sequence of prayers, including 5 sets of 10 "Hail Mary" prayers while meditating on different events in the lives of Jesus and Mary, all of which teach us about God's plan for our salvation. It can be tempting to look at the rosary as rote repetition of prayers, but that is not its design or purpose.

Instead, because the Rosary originates in Mary's lived experience, Pope St. John Paul II explains that it is by nature contemplative, as it is an "outpouring of love" that continually points to meditating on the saving acts of her Son. He says that the rosary is a way of allowing God to speak. This is especially true when you surround the prayer in silence, infuse it with the Word of God and reflect deeply on each "mystery" in the life of Christ and Mary.

> *"By its nature the recitation of the Rosary calls for a quiet rhythm and a lingering pace, helping the individual to meditate on the mysteries of the Lord's life as seen through the eyes of her who was closest to the Lord. In this way the unfathomable riches of these mysteries are disclosed." (Marialis Cultus, Apostolic Exhortation of Pope Paul VI, 1974)*

In this novena, you will find an intentionally meditative and contemplative approach to praying the rosary with daily reflections to allow the Holy Spirit to guide you along your life's path.

What is a 54-Day Rosary Novena?

A traditional novena is a prayer you say for nine days in a row. A 54-day novena is made up of six sets of novenas, which total 54 days of prayer. According to tradition, the 54-day novena comes from an appearance of Mary to a young girl in Naples, Italy who had asked for Mary's intercession in healing her from an incurable illness. Mary asked her to pray three novenas of the rosary in petition and then three novenas of the rosary in thanksgiving.

So, a 54-day novena is designed for you to spend the first 27 days/three novenas praying for a particular intention and the final 27 days/three novenas in thanksgiving -- whether or not your prayer was answered.

This novena is similar to the traditional 54-day rosary novena but also has some distinct differences. For example, I have reworded the laying of the roses at Mary's feet to correspond to the graces meditated on in the mystery. I have also changed a few rose colors, to have a different one each day.

Mother Mary, we offer to you:
- Monday, pale blue roses, to remind you of the joys of becoming and being the mother of Jesus.
- Tuesday, violet roses, to remind you of the sorrow and sacrifice of you and your Son.
- Wednesday, pure white roses, to remind you of the purity and light of eternity in heaven.
- Thursday, orange roses, to remind you of the dust of the earth over which you and your Son traveled during His ministry and also the wheat used to make the bread that becomes His Body.
- Friday, blood red roses, to remind you of the passion of your Son and His precious Blood.
- Saturday, pale pink roses, to remind you of the beauty of womanhood.
- Sunday, golden yellow roses, to remind you of the glories experienced by you and your Son.

Praying and Living the Rosary

Like a traditional 54-day novena, you will find daily prompts or reflections for how to meditate on each mystery within this book. Each week or so, there will be a different theme to the meditations.

Focus on pondering the mysteries, entering as deeply as you can, and less on the repetitive prayers. The "Hail Mary" prayers are there to serve as a guide to provide a length of time and a rhythm to the meditations. I find it helpful to set aside quiet time to sit in prayer as I do this. Sometimes I play a recorded version of the rosary, so I can focus on the meditations instead of what bead I am on. If this is still difficult or if you are not used to praying the rosary every day, consider focusing on just one or two mysteries and what God is saying to you in those.

I also encourage you to keep a journal. Write down the meditations that really speak to you and have meaning for you. Record what the Lord says to you. Then you will be able to go back and revisit them to continue to listen to how God is working through them and is transforming you.

In your meditations, always stay within Church teaching and Scripture. God can use your imagination to speak to you, but do not let it stray from God's revealed truth. I continually ask the Holy Spirit and Mary to guide my thoughts to keep them holy and on track.

Please have an intention when you pray. If you wish and are able to add some type of sacrifice with your prayer, such as fasting from something you enjoy, that will deepen and strengthen your prayer further.

I recommend beginning each rosary with a brief prayer of praise. This puts you in right relationship with God, our Creator, to Whom we owe everything. Then I petition the Holy Spirit for inspiration and ask for Mary's intercession.

I wrote this novena to begin on the Memorial of the Blessed Virgin Mary, Mother of the Church, which is the day after Pentecost. You may, of course, pray it at other times of the year, but some of the themes of the meditations line up with Church feast days if started on this date.

May you find blessings in this novena, and please know that my prayers are with you as you pray!

Barbara

Saying the Rosary Each Day for the Rosary Novena

1. Begin with the Sign of the Cross
2. Say the Prayer of Praise
3. Recite the Rosary Novena Prayer
4. Pray the Apostles' Creed
5. Offer the intention for the rosary and pray the Our Father
6. For an increase in faith, hope, and love, pray three Hail Marys
7. Pray the Glory Be
8. For each of the five mysteries
    a. Read the mystery reflection
    b. Pray the Our Father
    c. Pray ten Hail Marys
    d. Pray the Glory Be
    e. Pray the Fatima Prayer
    f. Lay the Roses at Mary's feet
9. Pray the Spiritual Communion
10. Conclude with prayers of your choice
    a. Hail Holy Queen
    b. Memorare
    c. Saint Michael Prayer
11. End with the Sign of the Cross

... *My Immaculate Heart will triumph* ...

Prayers for the Journey

1 and 11. Sign of the Cross:
In the name of the Father, and of the Son, and of the Holy Spirit. Amen.

2. Prayer of Praise:
I love you, and I praise you, God. I worship You in all things.

Mother Mary, be my guide. Journey with me, pray with me. Open my heart and mind to the mysteries of our Lord.

Holy Spirit, inspire me and help me to pray as I ought.

3. Rosary Novena Prayer:
Hail, Queen of the Most Holy Rosary, my Mother Mary, hail! At your feet I humbly pray and offer you a Crown of Roses, each Hail Mary a rose, each ten bound together with my petition for a particular grace…

(First 27 days in petition:)
…O Holy Queen, dispenser of God's graces, and Mother of all who invoke you, you cannot look upon my gift and fail to see its binding. As you receive my gift, so will you receive my petition; from your bounty you will give me the favor I so earnestly and trustingly seek. I despair of nothing that I ask of you. Show yourself my Mother!

(Last 27 days in thanksgiving:)
…O Holy Queen, dispenser of God's graces, and Mother of all who invoke you, you cannot look upon my gift and fail to see its binding. As you receive my gift, I kindly implore you to receive my thanksgiving. From your bounty, you have granted me the favor I so trustingly sought. You have truly shown yourself my Mother!

Prayers for the Journey

4. Apostles' Creed:
I believe in God, the Father almighty, Creator of heaven and earth, and in Jesus Christ, his only Son, our Lord, who was conceived by the Holy Spirit, born of the Virgin Mary, suffered under Pontius Pilate, was crucified, died and was buried; he descended into hell; on the third day he rose again from the dead; he ascended into heaven, and is seated at the right hand of God the Father almighty; from there he will come to judge the living and the dead.
I believe in the Holy Spirit, the holy catholic Church, the communion of saints, the forgiveness of sins, the resurrection of the body, and life everlasting.

5 and 8b. Our Father:
Our Father, who art in heaven, hallowed be thy name; thy kingdom come, thy will be done on earth as it is in heaven.
Give us this day our daily bread, and forgive us our trespasses, as we forgive those who trespass against us; and lead us not into temptation, but deliver us from evil.

6 and 8c. Hail Mary:
Hail, Mary, full of grace, the Lord is with thee.
Blessed art thou among women and blessed is the fruit of thy womb, Jesus.
Holy Mary, Mother of God, pray for us sinners, now and at the hour of our death.

7 and 8d. Glory Be:
Glory be to the Father and to the Son and to the Holy Spirit, as it was in the beginning is now, and ever shall be world without end.

8e. Fatima Prayer:
O my Jesus, forgive us our sins. Save us from the fires of hell. Lead all souls to heaven, especially those in most need of Thy mercy.

Prayers for the Journey

9. Spiritual Communion:
My Jesus, really present in the most Holy Sacrament of the altar, since I cannot now receive you under the Sacramental Veil, I beseech you, with a heart full of love and longing, to come spiritually into my soul through the Immaculate heart of Your most Holy Mother, and abide with me forever. You in me, and I in You, in time and eternity with Mary.

(First 27 days in petition:)
Sweet Mother Mary, I offer you this Spiritual Communion to bind my bouquets in a wreath to place upon your brow. O my Mother, look with favor upon my gift, and in your love obtain for me (specify request here). Amen.

(Last 27 days in thanksgiving:)
Sweet Mother Mary, I offer you this Spiritual Communion to bind my bouquets in a wreath to place upon your brow in thanksgiving for (specify request here) which in your love you have obtained for me. Amen.

10a. Hail Holy Queen
Hail, Holy Queen, Mother of Mercy,
our life, our sweetness and our hope.
To thee do we cry,
poor banished children of Eve.
To thee do we send up our sighs,
mourning and weeping in this valley of tears.
Turn then, most gracious advocate,
thine eyes of mercy toward us,
and after this, our exile,
show unto us the blessed fruit of thy womb, Jesus.
O clement, O loving,
O sweet Virgin Mary.
Pray for us, O Holy Mother of God,
That we may be made worthy of the promises of Christ.

Prayers for the Journey

10b. Memorare
Remember, O most gracious Virgin Mary, that never was it known that anyone who fled to thy protection, implored thy help, or sought thy intercession, was left unaided.
Inspired by this confidence I fly unto thee, O Virgin of virgins, my Mother.
To thee do I come, before thee I stand, sinful and sorrowful.
O Mother of the Word Incarnate, despise not my petitions, but in thy mercy hear and answer me.

10c. St. Michael Prayer
St. Michael the Archangel, defend us in battle. Be our protection against the wickedness and snares of the devil. May God rebuke him we humbly pray; and do thou, O Prince of the Heavenly host, by the power of God, cast into hell Satan and all the evil spirits who prowl about the world seeking the ruin of souls.

Week 1

    We begin living the rosary most fittingly on this memorial of the Blessed Virgin Mary, Mother of the Church. Let us pray together as the Church, for the Church, with the Mother of the Church. We stand with Mary as her children at the foot of the cross, ready for what awaits us next. We devote ourselves with one accord to prayer with the Mother of Jesus, and we do not fear, for we are helping to strike at the head of the serpent (see today's Mass readings).

    We go forth from celebrating Pentecost with the power of the Holy Spirit guiding us from within!

    Each week will have a different theme. We begin this first week by looking at Mary, her role in salvation history and also her presence in our lives. Let her guide you on this journey through the rosary. In the first few days we see where and how Mary is present in the mystery and what she is doing. She has invited you to share these moments with her. You will be experiencing them with her. Watch, listen, learn. Then at the end of the week we will look at where Mary is with you in the moments of your life.

    Thank you so much for joining me in this novena. Let us begin.

    Come, pray the rosary with me...

Day 1

First Joyful Mystery - The Annunciation

I am with Mary as she goes about her daily routine, this young girl completely dedicated to God. Whatever she does is for Him and with Him. Her openness to Him in all things is beautiful and attractive. For her, nothing is without meaning, nothing is without praise to Him. I see her loving God in everything she does.

She becomes aware of a presence that I cannot sense. She motions to me, wanting me to experience this with her. "Come," she says to me with an expectant look on her face. Then I see the angel appear...

First Joyful Mystery - Lay the Roses

Mother Mary, I bind these pale blue roses with a petition for the grace of openness to God and humbly lay this bouquet at your feet.

Second Joyful Mystery - The Visitation

Mary and I are both overjoyed at the angel's visit and announcement to her. She was beautiful before, but now there is a new glow about her that radiates from within. Her great happiness does not seem to be for herself, but for others - for me, for her people, for her expectant cousin. She wants so much to return the love that has been shown to her. We are preparing for the trip to visit Elizabeth. It will be long, but God's Son will be with us. We are ready. Come...

Second Joyful Mystery - Lay the Roses

Mother Mary, I bind these pale blue roses with a petition for the grace of charity and humbly lay this bouquet at your feet.

Third Joyful Mystery - The Birth of Jesus

We made the long trip to Bethlehem, with Mary so close to her time to deliver. I feel unworthy to be here at this time. She helps me to feel at ease, because she herself is always at peace, even in this dark, smelly stable. She radiates joy. There is a stillness in the air that is just as expectant as she is. Joseph feels it too. The Son of God is about to be born into the world and I am here! Mary knows it is time. She wants us near. Come...

Third Joyful Mystery - Lay the Roses

Mother Mary, I bind these pale blue roses with a petition for the grace of waiting patiently for God and humbly lay this bouquet at your feet.

Fourth Joyful Mystery - The Presentation in the Temple

We are in Jerusalem. Mary and Joseph are at the Temple to present Jesus and offer their sacrifice. It is also for Mary's purification. She miraculously bore God's Son. She is already pure but does not consider herself above the Law. Rather she is overjoyed at being here with her family and doing her duty to the Lord. I am in awe of this moment that she and Joseph allow me to share with them. I am hesitant. Mary motions me closer. "Come." We enter the Temple together...

Fourth Joyful Mystery - Lay the Roses

Mother Mary, I bind these pale blue roses with a petition for the grace of purity and humbly lay this bouquet at your feet.

Fifth Joyful Mystery - Finding of the Child Jesus in the Temple

We are leaving Jerusalem after celebrating Passover. There is great happiness among our group of travelers. We celebrated together and now return home together. Looking at Mary I see concern on her face. She is usually always so peaceful. It causes me to worry. I can see she is deep in thought and in her communication with God. Joseph is by her side. She motions for me to come...

Fifth Joyful Mystery - Lay the Roses

Mother Mary, I bind these pale blue roses with a petition for the grace of reliance on God and humbly lay this bouquet at your feet.

Day 2

First Sorrowful Mystery - The Agony in the Garden

The air feels heavy tonight. Mary is upset. We are together in the house in Jerusalem. The Passover feast was different this year. It did not feel like a celebration. I am anxious and I'm not sure why. Mary is preoccupied. She feels pain, I can see that. Jesus went to the garden to pray with His apostles. Mary is here with me, but I know she is with Him in spirit and that something is very wrong. He must be in pain, because she can feel it too. They are connected in a way that I do not understand, but it is very strong and very powerful. It fills the air. I can almost sense it too...

First Sorrowful Mystery - Lay the Roses

Mother Mary, I bind these violet roses with a petition for the grace of connection with God and humbly lay this bouquet at your feet.

Second Sorrowful Mystery - The Scourging at the Pillar

We have heard that Jesus has been arrested. John came to tell Mary, and she allows me to accompany them. She wants to see Him. He has been taken before the Jewish leaders and before Pilate. We push our way through the crowd of people. Pilate has just ordered that Jesus be scourged. He is dragged by the guards and bound to a pillar. His clothing is taken from Him to expose the bare skin. The men hold the scourges to which are fastened sharp pieces of metal and bone. Mary's eyes grow wide. John and I grab her arms and hold tightly to her as the men begin...

Second Sorrowful Mystery - Lay the Roses

Mother Mary, I bind these violet roses with a petition for the grace of mortification and humbly lay this bouquet at your feet.

Third Sorrowful Mystery - The Crowning with Thorns

Even though He is bloodied and in intense pain, Jesus is harshly treated by the guards. We watch as He continues to be wounded, ridiculed, and mocked. Mary refuses to take her eyes off Him, willing her presence and her love upon Him. I can see that she aches to run to Him. I also see her praying softly. I think she is asking for relief for her Son, but no. She prays for the men who harm Him, for their souls, their forgiveness for denying that He is truly a King...

Third Sorrowful Mystery - Lay the Roses

Mother Mary, I bind these violet roses with a petition for the grace of fear of the Lord and humbly lay this bouquet at your feet.

Fourth Sorrowful Mystery - The Carrying of the Cross

Despite the suffering that her heart endured watching her Son be tortured, Mary is determined to be close to Him. He is paraded down the street, the heavy wood upon His back. John urges her away from the gruesome scene, but she pulls forward. She needs to be closer to Him. She grabs my hand, and we wind our way through the narrow, crowded streets. Finally, there is an opening, and she pushes forward to be near the path of her Son. Here He comes, barely able to stay on His feet. I notice the moment when Jesus and Mary see each other. Their eyes connect. So many unspoken words pass between them. Comfort, compassion, strength, love. It is so intense that I feel like I should turn away and let this moment be just for them, but I cannot...

Fourth Sorrowful Mystery - Lay the Roses

Mother Mary, I bind these violet roses with a petition for the grace of perseverance and humbly lay this bouquet at your feet.

Fifth Sorrowful Mystery - The Crucifixion

The unthinkable has happened. Jesus has been crucified. My legs are weak, my tears are spent. My whole being feels filled with horror. When I think that I can bear it no longer, that I might run away in fear and terror, I look at Mary as we stand on the hill. There she is, those quiet prayers on her lips, remaining strong and determined. She is extremely sorrowful, yet it seems that she is giving that sorrow right to God. I can almost see her heart beating upward, the love pouring forth...

Fifth Sorrowful Mystery - Lay the Roses

Mother Mary, I bind these violet roses with a petition for the grace of sacrificial love and humbly lay this bouquet at your feet.

Day 3

The First Glorious Mystery - The Resurrection

I am with Mary in her room early on the morning of the third day since Jesus' death, waiting and praying. She allows me to share in her sorrows. But her grief is different from mine. She is mourning but also seems to be anticipating, waiting in faith and trust and hope. She continues to pray, giving herself to God, as she has always done.

She is not going to the tomb with the other women to anoint the body. She has asked me to stay with her. Mary knows her Son is not there. Her trust in God and His plan is perfect. And so, she waits with me.

I know that she is always with me, especially in my darkest moments. She waits with me with hope and expectation, because she knows God is doing something remarkable.

Suddenly her countenance changes. There is a glow in the room as her face fills with joy. "Come and see Him," she says to me...

First Glorious Mystery - Lay the Roses

Mother Mary, I bind these pure white roses with a petition for the grace of faith and humbly lay this bouquet at your feet.

Second Glorious Mystery - Ascension

There is a large gathering. Jesus is leading His disciples out of the city. I search for Mary. She locks eyes with me and motions for me to follow. I want to know what is happening. She smiles, takes my hand. "Come, you shall see." Jesus leads us up the Mount of Olives.

Mary always accompanies me with Jesus in all I do. There are different mountaintop experiences in life. They can be amazing and are often

unexpected. God always gives what I need. But I have to let Him surprise me. I need to be open and not have expectations.

Here, there is great anticipation. What will Jesus do next? Mary and I walk together. I sense excitement yet also a little sadness within her. I wonder why. Jesus turns to us and begins to speak...

Second Glorious Mystery - Lay the Roses

Mother Mary, I bind these pure white roses with a petition for the grace of accompaniment and humbly lay this bouquet at your feet.

Third Glorious Mystery - Descent of the Holy Spirit

Jesus has risen into the clouds. We are all amazed. We watch with eager anticipation for Him to return. Mary takes my hand. "Come," she says to me and turns to leave. There is joy but also a longing on her face. I start to follow her, yet no one else leaves. Why do not we wait for Jesus? He will be back, right? Others are still looking up at the sky.

Mary does not leave me standing and waiting uselessly. She guides me to where I need to go, especially to prayer and to listen to God and to receive what He wants to give me.

The others eventually follow, and we go to the upper room in the city. Mary leads us in prayer. She never seems to stop praying, no matter what she is doing. Her whole body prays. She teaches me to pray, helping me to persevere, how to be open to the Holy Spirit. For days we wait and pray. On the ninth day, Mary's prayers seem to intensify. Suddenly she rises, her eyes looking upward, her hands upraised. Something begins to happen...

Third Glorious Mystery - Lay the Roses

Mother Mary, I bind these pure white roses with a petition for the grace of continual prayer and humbly lay this bouquet at your feet.

Fourth Glorious Mystery - Assumption of Mary

It has been many years since the incredible events in Jerusalem. Jesus' followers have gone to preach His Good News to all who will listen. It has been an amazing and frightening time. I visit Mary and John. She is happy to see me as always and embraces me. "Come," she says to me as she invites me inside the home. There is a peace and quietness about her. I see something else too, that longing that I sensed when Jesus ascended. She misses Him. We all do. His Spirit has been with us, but she still misses being with Him. She seems ready...

Hers is the path that I must follow. As always, she leads the way to Jesus and eternal life. She waits for me to join her someday as she watches over me, protecting me.

Fourth Glorious Mystery - Lay the Roses

Mother Mary, I bind these pure white roses with a petition for the grace of longing for heaven and humbly lay this bouquet at your feet.

Fifth Glorious Mystery - Coronation of Mary

I can't believe she is gone, yet I am happy for her to be reunited with her Son. She has left us, but I still sense her presence somehow. I feel her calling. She wants to share one more thing with me. I can hear her faint whisper, "Come and watch." My vision changes and I can see her now, more beautiful than ever...

As she watches over me from heaven, she intercedes for me from before the throne of God. She takes my meager offerings and presents them perfectly to Him in the way that only she can.

Fifth Glorious Mystery - Lay the Roses

Mother Mary, I bind these pure white roses with a petition for the grace of heavenly intercession and humbly lay this bouquet at your feet.

Day 4

The First Luminous Mystery - Baptism of Jesus in the Jordan River

Mary and I are walking along the edge of a hill. I realize that we are looking down on the Jordan River. People have gathered around. I recognize John the Baptizer with his rough clothing of camel hair. He is preaching, inviting people into the water. I see someone moving toward John through the crowd. It is Jesus! He approaches John. Despite the distance from us, I can hear the conversation quite plainly. Mary looks at me and smiles and nods toward the river, explaining what I am seeing.

Mary, you were with me as I began my life as a Christian at my baptism. You are with me today as I strive to live out my baptismal promises. Help me to understand what Jesus' baptism means for me...

First Luminous Mystery – Lay the Roses

Mother Mary, I bind these orange roses with a petition for the grace of unity with God and humbly lay this bouquet at your feet.

Second Luminous Mystery – Wedding at Cana

I am excited to have been invited to attend a wedding in Cana with Mary and Jesus. Mary knows the young couple being united and has a special place of honor. She has chosen me to sit with her. She watches over everything, noticing all, giving her full attention to those she is with.

So it is with me too. I have invited her into my life, and she is here with me through everything. She notices my needs and asks Jesus to help me, sometimes without me even realizing it...

Second Luminous Mystery – Lay the Roses

Mother Mary, I bind these orange roses with a petition for the grace of intercession and humbly lay this bouquet at your feet.

Third Luminous Mystery – Proclamation of the Kingdom of God

Mary, the other women, and I accompany Jesus at times during His years of ministry. What a gift to hear Him teach about God and to watch Him heal with a word or a touch. Mary explains it all to me, what He is doing and why. She knows Him better than anyone. She helps me to understand Him too.

I know that I can pray to her asking for help when I do not understand what God is doing in my life or what He is trying to teach me. And she always leads me to Jesus...

Third Luminous Mystery – Lay the Roses

Mother Mary, I bind these orange roses with a petition for the grace of wisdom and humbly lay this bouquet at your feet.

Fourth Luminous Mystery – The Transfiguration

Mary and I are together outside. We see Jesus and three apostles walking out of town. I wonder where they are going. Mary knows what I am thinking. Somehow, she takes me there. We watch the scene from a distance in amazement.

Mary helps me to fully see and appreciate the divinity of her Son, God's Son, and how I can let His light illuminate and strengthen me...

Fourth Luminous Mystery – Lay the Roses

Mother Mary, I bind these orange roses with a petition for the grace of attentiveness to the presence of God and humbly lay this bouquet at your feet.

Fifth Luminous Mystery – The Institution of the Eucharist

Mary wants to share a significant moment in the life of Jesus with me. Only a few were there initially, but we are all able to share in this at every Mass, because there really is just one Holy Sacrifice of the Mass. I can tell this is very special to Mary, to be able to be united with her Son in this way, welcoming Him once more into her being, the same Body that she carried within her womb. Her tears of love and joy move me to tears.

I ask her to be with me when I receive her Son in Holy Communion so I can be a more fitting tabernacle for Him as she was...

Fifth Luminous Mystery – Lay the Roses

Mother Mary, I bind these orange roses with a petition for the grace of thanksgiving and humbly lay this bouquet at your feet.

Day 5

First Sorrowful Mystery – The Agony in the Garden

Life has its share of worries and difficulties, struggles and sufferings. I am in the garden praying, pouring out my concerns to God. Mary is there too. She feels my pain and my hurt as she did with Jesus. She is praying for me and with me. She is comforting me, ministering to me, mothering me...

First Sorrowful Mystery – Lay the Roses

Mother Mary, I bind these blood red roses with a petition for the grace of accompaniment and humbly lay this bouquet at your feet.

Second Sorrowful Mystery – The Scourging at the Pillar

Sometimes I feel like life is beating me up, like it is a battle that I am losing. Over and over, hardships come at me, and I do not think I can bear the pain. Mary wants to shield me from the blows that come at me. I allow her. With her protective mantle around me, she pulls me close...

Second Sorrowful Mystery - Lay the Roses

Mother Mary, I bind these blood red roses with a petition for the grace of spiritual protection and humbly lay this bouquet at your feet.

Third Sorrowful Mystery - The Crowning with Thorns

How many times have I felt embarrassed, humiliated, mocked, or ridiculed? Others may try to make me feel small and worthless. The devil attempts this all the time, pushing those thorns into my head. Mary gently lifts the crown of thorns from me and replaces it with one similar to her own beautiful crown, affirming me as a child of God and as her child...

Third Sorrowful Mystery - Lay the Roses

Mother Mary, I bind these red roses with a petition for the grace of affirmation and humbly lay this bouquet at your feet.

Fourth Sorrowful Mystery - The Carrying of the Cross

The weight of my struggles feels too heavy for me to endure at times. Jesus asks me to pick up my cross and follow Him, but I am not sure I am able. Mary is with me though. She is my Simon of Cyrene, helping me along the way. She encourages me as she did her Son...

Fourth Sorrowful Mystery - Lay the Roses

Mother Mary, I bind these blood red roses with a petition for the grace of encouragement and humbly lay this bouquet at your feet.

Fifth Sorrowful Mystery - The Crucifixion

I have a cross that is mine and that I have to embrace. Jesus embraced His for me. I embrace mine for Him. Mary in all her strength and faith and trust stood by her Son. She is by me too, giving me her help as all good mothers do. She reminds me that I am hers and that I am loved...

Fifth Sorrowful Mystery - Lay the Roses

Mother Mary, I bind these blood red roses with a petition for the grace of love and humbly lay this bouquet at your feet.

Day 6

First Joyful Mystery - The Annunciation

When I arise ready to begin a new day, Mary encourages me to spend some quiet time with the Lord first, before anything else. I talk to Him about my day and entrust everything to Him. I surrender it all to Him. I ask for help to be able to give Him my yes more fully, my "Fiat" like Mary. I know I can encounter Him in every situation. Mary helps me to be open to Him as she was, as she is. I want to receive Him in whatever way He chooses to announce Himself to me today...

First Joyful Mystery - Lay the Roses

Mother Mary, I bind these pale pink roses with the grace of surrender and humbly lay this bouquet at your feet.

Second Joyful Mystery - The Visitation

Once again Mary is with me as I go forth in love to serve God through the service of others, especially those to whom I am closest. Since I am learning to be more open to Him, I am aware of when He wants to send me on a mission different from what I had planned. Like Mary, I do not complain but go in haste to help where I can...

Second Joyful Mystery - Lay the Roses

Mother Mary, I bind these pale pink roses with a petition for the grace of openness and humbly lay this bouquet at your feet.

Third Joyful Mystery - The Birth of Jesus

Mary and Joseph experience many unexpected events in their lives. They are obedient to what they have to do. They accompany me along the unexpected

paths where my life's journey can take me. I welcome their intercession, help, and guidance. With them, I celebrate the joys that come from my yes to God and praise God for His quiet, gentle presence...

Third Joyful Mystery - Lay the Roses

Mother Mary, I bind these pale pink roses with a petition for the grace of joy and humbly lay this bouquet at your feet.

Fourth Joyful Mystery - The Presentation in the Temple

Mary and Joseph also show me how to fulfill my obligation to God in worship. I owe everything to God, but especially my praise and reverence. I let them guide my prayer times but especially at the Holy Sacrifice of the Mass. That is my highest form of prayer. Mary shows me how I can pray the Mass with her, with all the saints, with the Church...

Fourth Joyful Mystery - Lay the Roses

Mother Mary, I bind these pale pink roses with a petition for the grace of worship of God and humbly lay this bouquet at your feet.

Fifth Joyful Mystery - Finding of the Child Jesus in the Temple

Mary and Joseph understand what it is like to suffer and to undergo hardship and disappointment. They draw strength from God but also from each other. I can receive fortitude and help from their intercession. They walk with me when I need to turn and go a different direction, and they ponder and pray with me when I do not understand God's ways. Like Mary, I keep these things in my heart.

Fifth Joyful Mystery - Lay the Roses

Mother Mary, I bind these pale pink roses with a petition for the grace of understanding and humbly lay this bouquet at your feet.

Week 2

Happy Solemnity of the Most Holy Trinity!

As the *Catechism of the Catholic Church* states in paragraph 234, "The mystery of the Most Holy Trinity is the central mystery of Christian faith and life. It is the mystery of God in himself. It is therefore the source of all the other mysteries of faith, the light that enlightens them. It is the most fundamental and essential teaching."

God wishes to share Himself with us and invites us into His life of a Trinitarian communion of Love. "God himself is an eternal exchange of love, Father, Son and Holy Spirit, and he has destined us to share in that exchange." (CCC 221)

Most fittingly, the focus in our meditations this week will be the presence of God. God the Father Himself will be guiding our meditations, so they are written as if He is speaking directly to you. Let Him take you by the hand and show you His presence.

In the reflections this week, you will notice some repetition. The meditations for most of the mysteries are continuous. For example, the Father's words on Sunday in the glorious mysteries are copied on Wednesday, and then the new message is added below that in italics. Wednesday's meditation is an extension of what He says on Sunday. So, the glorious mystery meditation (Sunday and Wednesday) is one continuous thought spread out over those two days. This happens again with the joyful (Monday and Saturday) and the sorrowful (Tuesday and Friday.) This does not happen in the luminous mysteries on Thursday because they are only prayed on one day. This format occurs again in week 6.

    Come, let us pray with the Father...

Day 7

The First Glorious Mystery - The Resurrection

Come, my child. This is your Father here to guide you. Take My hand. See My Son, His Body fully alive, resurrected for you, for your future glory to new life. See His hands where the nails once held Him to the cross. They are spread wide once again welcoming you in love. See the feet, also pierced, ready to journey with you. The crown He wears now has no thorns. See Him in His glory!

First Glorious Mystery - Lay the Roses

Mother Mary, I bind these golden yellow roses with a petition for the grace of glorifying God and humbly lay this bouquet at your feet.

Second Glorious Mystery - Ascension

Come, my child. See My Son as He stands on the mountaintop, pausing to be with the ones He loves before returning to Me. He has left so much for the world. Will the world use what it has been given? He offers a blessing to all. See this blessing spread across the whole world as He ascends. His earthly mission continues in you.

Second Glorious Mystery - Lay the Roses

Mother Mary, I bind these golden yellow roses with a petition for the grace of mission and humbly lay this bouquet at your feet.

Third Glorious Mystery - Descent of the Holy Spirit

Come, my child, to the upper room. See My Spirit as He enters. My Presence fills the room. I am the Lord, your God. Feel My Presence. Know that I am with you. The fire you see is a manifestation of the power I place in

these disciples. The presence of God goes into each one, but each has their own tongue of fire. Everyone is called to their own mission, so they are given what they each need to accomplish that. The Holy Spirit empowers them to go forth.

Third Glorious Mystery - Lay the Roses

Mother Mary, I bind these golden yellow roses with a petition for the grace of the power of God and humbly lay this bouquet at your feet.

Fourth Glorious Mystery - Assumption of Mary

Come, my child. See my daughter. All that has been given to her is My doing. She was chosen by Me to be the Immaculate one for My Son. We do not leave her body that was made so perfectly. We bring her back to Us. Her existence did not end, it was changed, transformed to the heavenly realm.

Fourth Glorious Mystery - Lay the Roses

Mother Mary, I bind these golden yellow roses with a petition for the grace of perfection and humbly lay this bouquet at your feet.

Fifth Glorious Mystery - Coronation of Mary

Come, my child. See your Queen who loves you as your heavenly Mother. All of heaven rejoices at her coronation. But she truly became a queen in her service to Me and humanity by the gift of herself. She lived her queenship through her love.

Fifth Glorious Mystery - Lay the Roses

Mother Mary, I bind these golden yellow roses with a petition for the grace of service and humbly lay this bouquet at your feet.

Day 8

First Joyful Mystery - The Annunciation

God the Father: *Come, my child. See Mary, the perfect creature. My presence fills her entire being. She lives in the world - interacting, loving, and serving - all with her Creator in mind, who is Love. All she does is in light of eternity, all for Love, with Love, in Love. Her "yes" is because of her Love, her God. See the Holy Spirit overshadow her at her fiat. She chooses the way of Love. See My Son begin to grow in her.*

First Joyful Mystery - Lay the Roses

Mother Mary, I bind these pale blue roses with a petition for the grace of love of God and humbly lay this bouquet at your feet.

Second Joyful Mystery - The Visitation

Come, my child. See the joy in Mary. Being completely open to God produces this. She shares in the joy of others. Life is not a competition but a cooperation in love. Her concern is not for herself, for she knows I am taking care of her. She does not fully understand how yet. Joseph still has to give his fiat. She lets her joy carry her through the long journey. She arrives tired yet does not complain. Rather, she gives her canticle of praise.

Second Joyful Mystery - Lay the Roses

Mother Mary, I bind these pale blue roses with a petition for the grace of joy and humbly lay this bouquet at your feet.

Third Joyful Mystery - The Birth of Jesus

Come, my child. See Mary and Joseph. They stand looking at their home before leaving for Bethlehem. They know that they won't be returning for a while. Trips in this time were often long and arduous. But their trust in Me is complete, so they are blessed in a special way. They set off not knowing the hardships that await. But glory also awaits them. They have each other for support and companionship.

Third Joyful Mystery - Lay the Roses

Mother Mary, I bind these pale blue roses with a petition for the grace of trust and humbly lay this bouquet at your feet.

Fourth Joyful Mystery - The Presentation in the Temple

Come, my child. See Mary and Joseph again. Everything is different for them now, because they see things through the lens of parenthood to My Son. Their lives are centered on God and the care of Jesus. All first-born were presented at the Temple and then ransomed back with a sacrifice. The very center of their lives, their reason for being, is offered to Me, and I give Him back to them. With My Son's presence here, God's glory once again fills the Temple. Only a few realized this at the time. I share this with you now.

Fourth Joyful Mystery - Lay the Roses

Mother Mary, I bind these pale blue roses with a petition for the grace of giving all to God and humbly lay this bouquet at your feet.

Fifth Joyful Mystery - Finding of the Child Jesus in the Temple

Come, my child. See the Holy Family. The worship of God is central to their lives. Travel to Jerusalem could mean a complete trip taking weeks. But they do not see this as an inconvenience. To serve their God comes first. This is foremost within their family and for their whole community.
Joseph and Mary taught My Son well. Jesus was a human child in all ways and had to learn. All could see that God is their priority. Faith is to be lived as an individual, a family, and a community. Jesus had a strong connection

to the Temple and to His mission and identity, even at a young age. His connection to Me, His Father, is what is most important to Him.

Fifth Joyful Mystery - Lay the Roses

Mother Mary, I bind these pale blue roses with a petition for the grace of learning and humbly lay this bouquet at your feet.

Day 9

First Sorrowful Mystery - The Agony in the Garden

Come, my child. See My Son in prayer in the garden. He knows the importance of time with Me. As a human, this was necessary for Him. As My Son, the Second Person of the Trinity, we are always connected. This time is especially difficult for Him. He suffers much out of love for you. As He suffers, so do I suffer. Our Hearts together ache for the redemption of your soul.

First Sorrowful Mystery - Lay the Roses

Mother Mary, I bind these violet roses with a petition for the grace of compassion and humbly lay this bouquet at your feet.

Second Sorrowful Mystery - The Scourging at the Pillar

Come, my child. See My Son who is in great agony again. This causes me pain. But it is for you: to cleanse you, to heal you. By His wounds you are healed. Accept this healing. Do not let it be in vain. It is difficult to watch. But it should give you hope, because it brings you life.

Second Sorrowful Mystery - Lay the Roses

Mother Mary, I bind these violet roses with a petition for the grace of healing and humbly lay this bouquet at your feet.

Third Sorrowful Mystery - The Crowning with Thorns

Come, my child. See My Son being mocked and ridiculed. They spit on the King of the Universe. Some deny His Kingship. Some realize it but are unmoved. This is even worse. Jesus is a humble, gentle, and loving King. How can they attempt to humiliate One Who is all humility? So many

people worship other things, living their lives praying to idols. Come to know Jesus as your King Who loves you.

Third Sorrowful Mystery - Lay the Roses

Mother Mary, I bind these violet roses with a petition for the grace of humility and humbly lay this bouquet at your feet.

Fourth Sorrowful Mystery - The Carrying of the Cross

Come, my child. See My Son as He is weighed down by the cross so heavy with sin. It is very difficult for Him, yet He carries it out of love for you. He took it up not begrudgingly but willingly. He embraces that cross to save you. Thank Him. Like Veronica lovingly does, offer to wipe His face.

Fourth Sorrowful Mystery - Lay the Roses

Mother Mary, I bind these violet roses with a petition for the grace of thanksgiving and humbly lay this bouquet at your feet.

Fifth Sorrowful Mystery - The Crucifixion

Come, my child. See My Son in His ultimate act of love for you. He has been crucified and is dying on the cross. He Who is without sin took on your sin for your salvation. Kneel before Him in worship and adoration.

Fifth Sorrowful Mystery - Lay the Roses

Mother Mary, I bind these violet roses with a petition for the grace of adoration and humbly lay this bouquet at your feet.

Day 10

The First Glorious Mystery - The Resurrection

Come, my child. This is your Father here to guide you. Take My hand. See My Son, His Body fully alive, resurrected for you, for your future glory to new life. See His hands where the nails once held Him to the cross. They are spread wide once again welcoming you in love. See the feet, also pierced, ready to journey with you. The crown He wears now has no thorns. See Him in His glory!

My child, know that this was all for you. Jesus died and rose to glory, so you can do the same. Let me take you to the tomb. Yes, it is very dark. I want you to experience this. You need to encounter these times of darkness and death before the resurrection. This is the way that it is. Do not be discouraged when you are in this phase. I am here with you, holding your hand. The light is coming. Look, you can see it beginning. The light of My Son bringing you new life, life to the world.

First Glorious Mystery - Lay the Roses

Mother Mary, I bind these pure white roses with a petition for the grace of new life and humbly lay this bouquet at your feet.

Second Glorious Mystery - Ascension

Come, my child. See My Son as He stands on the mountaintop, pausing to be with the ones He loves before returning to Me. He has left so much for the world. Will the world use what it has been given? He offers a blessing to all. See this blessing spread across the whole world as He ascends. His earthly mission is not over. It continues in you.

Come, my child. Draw close. At times you may feel as if Jesus has left you, that God is not with you. This is never true. I created you. I created everything. I am a part of everything. I am always there, in everything. Yes, there will be discouragement and disappointment in life. But your God is in every situation, giving you little nudges of encouragement. Look for them. Ask Me for them. I want to show you My Presence.

Second Glorious Mystery - Lay the Roses

Mother Mary, I bind these pure white roses with a petition for the grace of seeking God and humbly lay this bouquet at your feet.

Third Glorious Mystery - Descent of the Holy Spirit

Come, my child, to the upper room. See My Spirit as He enters. My Presence fills the room. I am the Lord, your God. Feel My Presence. Know that I Am with you. The fire you see is a manifestation of the power I place in these disciples. The presence of God goes into each one, but each has their own tongue of fire. Everyone is called to their own mission, so they are given what they each need to accomplish that. The Holy Spirit empowers them to go forth.

My child, I am with you too and have come to set you ablaze. Do not be afraid, for My Presence is Love. Let My Spirit ignite your heart, inflame your mind, enkindle your soul. Do all things with My power living in you.

Third Glorious Mystery - Lay the Roses

Mother Mary, I bind these pure white roses with a petition for the grace of inspiration and humbly lay this bouquet at your feet.

Fourth Glorious Mystery - Assumption of Mary

Come, my child. See my daughter. All that has been given to her is My doing. She was chosen by Me to be the Immaculate one for My Son. We do not leave her body that We made so perfectly. We bring her back to Us. Her existence did not end, it was changed, transformed to the heavenly realm.

My child, you too are destined for heavenly existence with Me. At the end of your earthly life, you will join Us. This is not something to fear, but to anticipate with hope. Being with your God in heaven forever is your fulfillment.

Fourth Glorious Mystery - Lay the Roses

Mother Mary, I bind these pure white roses with a petition for the grace of hope and humbly lay this bouquet at your feet.

Fifth Glorious Mystery - Coronation of Mary

Come, my child. See your Queen who loves you as your heavenly Mother. All of heaven rejoices at her coronation. But she truly became a queen in her service to Me and humanity by the gift of herself. She lived her queenship through her love.

My child, you are given nobility as well. As My child you are a part of My royal family. Reflect this to the world. Your destination is My kingdom in heaven, but you are to live out your royalty here and now. Live as a child of the King, as My beloved. When the world tries to make you doubt this truth, ask and I will remind you. I will show you the crown you will someday wear.

Fifth Glorious Mystery - Lay the Roses

Mother Mary, I bind these pure white roses with a petition for the grace of nobility and humbly lay this bouquet at your feet.

Day 11

The First Luminous Mystery - Baptism of Jesus in the Jordan River

Come, my child. See My Son. He descends into the waters of baptism, the waters of humankind, to take on all of humanity with all of its sins. He accepts this upon Himself. He plunges into the waters to retrieve you. You can feel overwhelmed under the weight of life. He penetrates the chaos and latches on to you. Your Jesus pulls you up with Him. As you rise from the waters, you both gasp for air. I, your God, fill you with My Breath of Life. Breathe Me in. Welcome Me as I fill you with My Spirit. Feel My Presence as I rejoice over you and call you my beloved.

First Luminous Mystery - Lay the Roses

Mother Mary, I bind these orange roses with a petition for the grace of blessedness and humbly lay this bouquet at your feet.

Second Luminous Mystery - Wedding at Cana

Come, my child. See My family represented here at Cana. Every family is my family. I have created man and woman with a special purpose. The unity in Holy Matrimony is sacred because it is a joining of three - man, woman, and God. Marriage is a covenant we make together. The children that arise from this union are given by Me. This reflects your God, the Holy Trinity. The perpetual Love between the Father and the Son is the Spirit. This is why your family is so holy and why the enemy tries to attack it. See, just as in Cana, your family is not alone. All of heaven is with you supporting you. Jesus, Mary, and the saints are here for you ready to supply what you need. I Am with you. Welcome Our love and help.

Second Luminous Mystery - Lay the Roses

Mother Mary, I bind these orange roses with a petition for the grace of heavenly unity and humbly lay this bouquet at your feet.

Third Luminous Mystery - Proclamation of the Kingdom of God

Come, my child. See My Son as He ministers to the world, as He brings God to the world. This is the Good News. He is here to reveal Our Presence in a new way. The Kingdom of Heaven is at hand. Listen to Him; learn from Him; be touched by Him; be healed by Him; be transformed by Him. Encounter with God should change you.

Third Luminous Mystery - Lay the Roses

Mother Mary, I bind these orange roses with a petition for the grace of encounter and humbly lay this bouquet at your feet.

Fourth Luminous Mystery - The Transfiguration

Come, my child. See My Son Transfigured in all His Glory. Be still and see Him...

I am present within Him. The Holy Spirit is present within Him. Our Light shines forth from Him. Bask in the Light of Our Love...

The Most Holy Trinity is within and surrounding you. Now carry Us with you back down the mountain.

Fourth Luminous Mystery - Lay the Roses

Mother Mary, I bind these orange roses with a petition for the grace of God's Light and humbly lay this bouquet at your feet.

Fifth Luminous Mystery - The Institution of the Eucharist

Come, my child. See My Son in this holy meal, the Eucharist. See Him lifted up for you. Truly see Him, for it <u>is</u> Him. We are also with Him, the Father and the Holy Spirit. What a great gift Jesus gives to you, the gift of Himself. Receive Him; welcome Him. And truly show Him Thanksgiving by letting His Presence transform you.

Fifth Luminous Mystery - Lay the Roses

Mother Mary, I bind these orange roses with a petition for the grace of union with Jesus and humbly lay this bouquet at your feet.

Day 12

First Sorrowful Mystery - The Agony in the Garden

Come, my child. See My Son in prayer in the garden. He knows the importance of time with Me. As a human, this was necessary for Him. As My Son, the Second Person of the Trinity, we cannot be apart. This time is especially difficult for Him. He suffers much out of love for you. As He suffers, so do I suffer. Our Hearts together ache for the redemption of your soul.

My child, I long for connection with you. Come to Me in prayer. When you are in your agony, I will console you. I unite Myself to you. We will experience it together. Tell me what troubles you. Open your heart to me. I Am with you.

First Sorrowful Mystery - Lay the Roses

Mother Mary, I bind these blood red roses with a petition for the grace of consolation and humbly lay this bouquet at your feet.

Second Sorrowful Mystery - The Scourging at the Pillar

Come, my child. See My Son who is in great agony again. This causes me pain. But it is for you: to cleanse you, to heal you. By His wounds you are healed. Accept this healing. Do not let it be in vain. It is difficult to watch. But it should give you hope, because it brings you life.

My child, I know you suffer as well. I created your body to enjoy the things of life but not in excess. It is overindulgence that harms. You are made for moderation. When the pleasures aren't constant, then they are appreciated more. Let Me help you, teach you balance and discipline in your life. Self-control will bring you the most freedom.

Second Sorrowful Mystery - Lay the Roses

Mother Mary, I bind these blood red roses with a petition for the grace of moderation and humbly lay this bouquet at your feet.

Third Sorrowful Mystery - The Crowning with Thorns

Come, my child. See My Son being mocked and ridiculed. They spit on the King of the Universe. Some deny His Kingship. Some realize it but are unmoved. This is even worse. Jesus is a humble, gentle, and loving king. How can they attempt to humiliate One Who is all humility? So many people worship other things, living their lives praying to idols. Come to know Jesus as your King Who loves you.

My child, you have one King. All else is meaningless. Worship God as you rightly should. Look at your life. Where do you put anything else before your God? We made you and hold you into being. I gave you your first breath. I will give you your last. Come, realize the joy and peace in honoring your God over everything else.

Third Sorrowful Mystery - Lay the Roses

Mother Mary, I bind these blood red roses with a petition for the grace of honoring God and humbly lay this bouquet at your feet.

Fourth Sorrowful Mystery - The Carrying of the Cross

Come, my child. See My Son as He is weighed down by the cross so heavy with sin. It is very difficult for Him, yet He carries it out of love for you. He took it up not begrudgingly but willingly. He embraces that cross to save you. Thank Him. Like Veronica lovingly does, offer to wipe His face.

My child, I know that you have a cross to bear that can be very difficult. It may seem too heavy or rough. At times the cross is of your own making.

Sometimes it is thrust upon you by others. I allow you to carry what you can. Embrace your cross willingly as My Son did, and allow Me to transform it and you.

Fourth Sorrowful Mystery - Lay the Roses

Mother Mary, I bind these blood red roses with a petition for the grace of reliance on God and humbly lay this bouquet at your feet.

Fifth Sorrowful Mystery - The Crucifixion

Come, my child. See My Son in His ultimate act of love for you. He has been crucified and is dying on the cross. He who is without sin took on your sin for your salvation. Kneel before Him in worship and adoration.

My child, Jesus has been crucified for your sake. He does not condemn you. I do not condemn you. We offer you mercy. We look on you with love. We did this out of love. For your salvation. Accept this gift to you. It is a free gift, but you must take it and use it. You can't hide it away. The gift of love is to be shared. Let your life reflect the love We have given to you. Let it change you.

Fifth Sorrowful Mystery - Lay the Roses

Mother Mary, I bind these blood red roses with a petition for the grace of mercy and humbly lay this bouquet at your feet.

Day 13

First Joyful Mystery - The Annunciation

God the Father says to me, "Come, my child. See Mary, the perfect creature. My presence fills her entire being. She lives in the world, interacting, loving, and serving, all with her Creator in mind, who is Love. All she does is in light of eternity, all for Love, with Love, in Love. Her "yes" is because of her Love, her God. See the Holy Spirit overshadow her at her Fiat. She chose the way of Love. See My Son begin to grow in her.

"My child, you are meant for this too. Sin makes it more difficult, but I created you for my Love as well. Open yourself to My Presence dwelling within. I Am there, in every part of you. Let Me guide you. Every time you say 'yes' to Me, you strengthen that connection with Me, and our bond becomes stronger."

First Joyful Mystery - Lay the Roses

Mother Mary, I bind these pale pink roses with a petition for the grace of obedience to God and humbly lay this bouquet at your feet.

Second Joyful Mystery - The Visitation

Come, my child. See the joy in Mary. Being completely open to God produces this. She shares in the joy of others. Life is not a competition but a cooperation in love. Her concern is not for herself, for she knows I am taking care of her. She does not fully understand how yet. Joseph still has to give his fiat. She lets her joy carry her through the long journey. She arrives tired yet does not complain. Rather, she gives her canticle of praise.

My child, this can be you on your journey. You can have this joy when you have God with you. The enemy wants you to be worried, anxious, and fearful. Your God wants peace and joy for you. The journey isn't easy, but I am with you. I want you to remember that. Then you will be filled with what you need to serve in love. You can take this to others.*

Second Joyful Mystery - Lay the Roses

Mother Mary, I bind these pale pink roses with a petition for the grace of peace and humbly lay this bouquet at your feet.

Third Joyful Mystery - The Birth of Jesus

Come, my child. See Mary and Joseph. They stand looking at their home before leaving for Bethlehem. They know that they won't be returning for a while. Trips in this time were often long and arduous. But their trust in Me is complete, so they are blessed in a special way. They set off not knowing the hardships that await. But glory also awaits them. They have each other for support and companionship.

My child, I see when you are hesitant to venture out into the unknown. You are unsure. Your trust may be lacking. You do not want the hardship and difficulty. Know that you do not go alone. It is through perseverance in these times that the glory is then revealed to you. Here, take my newborn Son and hold Him in your arms. Look at His face, which is also My face. Now look out at the sky and hear the angels proclaiming His birth. Here is your glory!

Third Joyful Mystery - Lay the Roses

Mother Mary, I bind these pale pink roses with a petition for the grace of the glory of God and humbly lay this bouquet at your feet.

Fourth Joyful Mystery - The Presentation of Jesus in the Temple

Come, my child. See Mary and Joseph again. Everything is different for them now, because they see things through the lens of parenthood to My Son. Their lives are centered on God and the care of Jesus. All first-born were presented at the Temple and then ransomed back with a sacrifice. The very center of their lives, their reason for being, is offered to Me, and I give Him back to them. With My Son's presence here, God's glory once again fills the Temple. Only a few realized this at the time. I share this with you now.

My child, I want you to live in light of My Son's presence in the world and in your life. See life through this lens. Give Me your all, everything. Offer it to Me. Then you will be able to recognize the Presence of God and the glory of God in the world. I reveal it in simple, quiet ways. Ask to be made aware.

Fourth Joyful Mystery - Lay the Roses

Mother Mary, I bind these pale pink roses with a petition for the grace of unveiling and humbly lay this bouquet at your feet.

Fifth Joyful Mystery - The Finding of the Child Jesus in the Temple

Come, my child. See the Holy Family. The worship of God is central to their lives. Travel to Jerusalem could mean a complete trip taking weeks. But they do not see this as an inconvenience. To serve their God comes first. This is foremost within their family and for their whole community.
Joseph and Mary taught My Son well. Jesus was a human child in all ways and had to learn. All could see that God is their priority. Faith is to be lived as an individual, a family, and a community. Jesus had a strong connection to the Temple and to His mission and identity, even at a young age. His connection to Me, His Father, is what is most important to Him.

My child, your connection to Me does not happen by chance or accident. I will it. I created you for it. I desire this union with you. But you need to work at it, foster it. Learn about Me, spend time with Me, and it will grow. Jesus needed to do this. Mary and Joseph did as well. It is a beautiful journey that I want to take with you. Open yourself up to Me and My Presence in your life.

Fifth Joyful Mystery - Lay the Roses

Mother Mary, I bind these pale pink roses with a petition for the grace of union with God and humbly lay this bouquet at your feet.

Week 3

Happy Solemnity of the Most Holy Body and Blood of Christ!

    Today we begin a new week in our novena. Last week God the Father guided us through the meditations. The members of the Holy Family will be leading us this week. Today, on the Solemnity of the Most Holy Body and Blood of Christ, it will be Jesus leading us. He will be our guide on two more days. Mary and Joseph will also be with us. The feasts of the week have determined the theme for the week, which will be the Hearts of Jesus, Mary, and Joseph.

    Also, this week's meditations continue through next Sunday. I feel that God the Father wants us to spend more time with Him to better understand His Heart, the Heart of the Father!

    God is the Father who created us. He formed every part of us and knows all aspects of our being. He really wants us to know Him as the ideal Father. The Fatherhood of God comes from the knowledge of God as our Creator. He made us, is present to us, cares for us, wants us to share in His being, and loves us. Let's allow our heavenly Father to show us what true Fatherhood and family really are.

The Holy Family says to us: come, pray the rosary with us...

Day 14

First Glorious Mystery - The Resurrection of Jesus

I am with you, your Jesus. We are outside the tomb. It is early in the morning of that first Easter. The angels have not yet rolled away the stone. The guards are asleep. All of heaven and earth await. Let us have this moment together.

See My Body resurrected for you. Look at My hands and feet from where the drops of My Precious Blood were shed for you. See the Light that emanates from My wounds.

Place your hand here on My chest. Feel the Heart, which was once stopped and empty. It now beats for you, pumping the Blood that gives you Life.

This I share with you. My Life for your life...

First Glorious Mystery - Lay the Roses

Mother Mary, I bind these golden yellow roses with a petition for the grace of fullness of life and humbly lay this bouquet at your feet.

Second Glorious Mystery - The Ascension of Jesus into Heaven

Come with your Jesus to the mount. Heaven anticipates My return. Look out at the world from up here. This part of My mission on earth is done, but many in the world still await Me. My Heart still beats with love for all of them. Now I will go to them through you. Your hands are My hands. Your feet are My feet. Take Me to them. Let our hearts beat together for love of them. I will be with you...

Second Glorious Mystery - Lay the Roses

Mother Mary, I bind these golden yellow roses with a petition for the grace of evangelization and humbly lay this bouquet at your feet.

Third Glorious Mystery - The Descent of the Holy Spirit

Your Jesus is with you as you pray. You want inspiration and help. Ask for My Presence, Our Presence, and We will come to you, your Father and the Holy Spirit and I. We are already with you, but We can fill you in a new way. Be open and receive the love from Our Hearts...

Third Glorious Mystery - Lay the Roses

Mother Mary, I bind these golden yellow roses with a petition for the grace of openness and humbly lay this bouquet at your feet.

Fourth Glorious Mystery - The Assumption of Mary

Watch with Me, your Jesus, as our perfect and beautiful Mother comes to Me in Heaven. All of heaven is joyful. Our Hearts overflow with love as we meet and embrace again. Can you feel it? Let our love flow into your heart also...

Fourth Glorious Mystery - Lay the Roses

Mother Mary, I bind these golden yellow roses with a petition for the grace of love and humbly lay this bouquet at your feet.

Fifth Glorious Mystery - The Coronation of Mary

Our Mother has come to accept her place as Queen of Heaven and earth. Rejoice with the saints and angels. Witness your Jesus place the crown on her head. When you pray to her, you are helping Me to place that crown. Feel the love that is heaven, that We have for all of humanity and creation. This love is also yours...

Fifth Glorious Mystery - Lay the Roses

Mother Mary, I bind these golden yellow roses with a petition for the grace of exultation and humbly lay this bouquet at your feet.

Day 15

First Joyful Mystery - The Annunciation

Now the birth of Jesus Christ took place in this way. When his mother Mary had been betrothed to Joseph, before they lived together she was found to be with child of the Holy Spirit; and her husband Joseph, being a just man and unwilling to put her to shame, resolved to send her away quietly. But as he considered this, behold, an angel of the Lord appeared to him in a dream, saying, "Joseph, son of David, do not fear to take Mary your wife, for that which is conceived in her is of the Holy Spirit; she will bear a son, and you shall call his name Jesus, for he will save his people from their sins." All this took place to fulfill what the Lord had spoken by the prophet: "Behold, a virgin shall conceive and bear a son, and his name shall be called 'Emmanuel' (which means, God with us). When Joseph woke from sleep, he did as the angel of the Lord commanded him; he took his wife into his home. ~Matthew 1:18-24

I, Joseph, learn of Mary being with child by the Holy Spirit. I am unsure what to do at first. I feel unworthy of her and what God is doing. I pray and wait on God to show me His will. My just heart is open to Him. I am asleep when His word comes to me. I am able to rest, because I trust in God to lead me. My wife and I talk about God's amazing plan. We both feel undeserving and overwhelmed yet full of joy that the Messiah is coming. Our realization of what is truly happening leads us to a great and pure bond with God and with each other. Our hearts are full. So begins our journey together...

First Joyful Mystery - Lay the Roses

Mother Mary, I bind these pale blue roses with a petition for the grace of faith in the Lord and humbly lay this bouquet at your feet.

Second Joyful Mystery - The Visitation

"And behold, your kinswoman Elizabeth in her old age has also conceived a son; and this is the sixth month with her who was called barren. For with God nothing will be impossible." And Mary said, "Behold, I am the handmaid of the Lord; let it be done to me according to your word." And the angel departed from her. In those days Mary arose and went with haste into the hill country, to a city of Judah, and she entered the house of Zechariah and greeted Elizabeth. ~Luke 1:36-40

I, Joseph, accompany Mary on her trip to the hill country. I will not allow Mary to travel alone. It is my heart's greatest desire to protect her and the Child. It is a considerable responsibility that I take very seriously. This is the first of many long trips that we take together. I am able to learn more about this amazing woman whom God allows to be my wife. I see the great love she has for God and for all others. I have come to understand and appreciate her respect for me. Our conversations and our prayers together are very special to me. I leave her with her cousin and eagerly await my return for her...

Second Joyful Mystery - Lay the Roses

Mother Mary, I bind these pale blue roses with a petition for the grace of companionship and humbly lay this bouquet at your feet.

Third Joyful Mystery - The Birth of Jesus

Joseph also went up from Galilee, from the city of Nazareth to Judea, to the city of David, which is called Bethlehem, because he was of the house and lineage of David, to be enrolled with Mary, his betrothed, who was with child. And while they were there, the time came for her to be delivered. And she gave birth to her first-born son and wrapped him in swaddling cloths, and laid him in a manger, because there was no place for them in the inn. And in that region, there were shepherds out in the field, keeping watch over their flock by night. And an angel of the Lord appeared to them, and the glory of the Lord shone around them, and they were filled with fear. And the angel said to them, "Be not afraid; for behold, I bring you good news of a great joy which will come to all the people; for to you is born this day in the city of David a Savior, who is Christ the Lord. And this will be a sign for you: you will find a babe wrapped in swaddling cloths and lying in a manger." And suddenly there was with the angel a multitude of the heavenly host praising God and saying, "Glory to God in the highest, and on earth peace among men with whom he is pleased!"

When the angels went away from them into heaven, the shepherds said to one another, "Let us go over to Bethlehem and see this thing that has happened, which the Lord has made known to us." And they went with haste, and found Mary and Joseph, and the babe lying in a manger. And when they saw it, they made known the saying which had been told them concerning this child; and all who heard it wondered at what the shepherds told them. But Mary kept all these things, pondering them in her heart. And the shepherds returned, glorifying and praising God for all they had heard and seen, as it had been told them. ~Luke 2:4-20

I, Joseph, am in awe of God and His workings, and I have such great admiration for my wife. We endured this trip, with Mary near the end of her pregnancy. She is so strong and faithful, knowing this is God's will for us. We go where the Lord takes us. My disappointment in our lowly circumstances in Bethlehem is overshadowed by God's glorious Child being born into our little family. God is not averse to coming in poverty and humility, so we embrace this life. And I, Joseph, am the first one to hold the Son of God in my arms. My heart can hardly contain its happiness. There is nothing more humbling than that...

Third Joyful Mystery - Lay the Roses

Mother Mary, I bind these pale blue roses with a petition for the grace of humility and humbly lay this bouquet at your feet.

Fourth Joyful Mystery - The Presentation in the Temple

And when the time came for their purification according to the law of Moses, they brought him up to Jerusalem to present him to the Lord (as it is written in the law of the Lord, "Every male that opens the womb shall be called holy to the Lord") and to offer a sacrifice according to what is said in the law of the Lord, "a pair of turtledoves, or two young pigeons." Now there was a man in Jerusalem, whose name was Simeon, and this man was righteous and devout, looking for the consolation of Israel, and the Holy Spirit was upon him. And it had been revealed to him by the Holy Spirit that he should not see death before he had seen the Lord's Christ. And inspired by the Spirit he came into the temple; and when the parents brought in the child Jesus, to do for him according to the custom of the law, he took him up in his arms and blessed God and said, "Lord, now let thou thy servant depart in peace, according to thy word; for mine eyes have seen thy salvation which thou hast prepared in the presence of all peoples, a light for revelation to the Gentiles, and for glory to thy people Israel."

And his father and his mother marveled at what was said about him; and Simeon blessed them and said to Mary his mother, "Behold, this child is set for the fall and rising of many in Israel, and for a sign that is spoken against (and a sword will pierce through your own soul also), that thoughts out of many hearts may be revealed." ~Luke 2:22-34

I, Joseph, take Mary and the Child to the Temple. We desire always to do our duty to God. Our Lord has blessed us, and we give our honor and worship to Him in fulfilling our obligations. The Child is God's own, yet the Father allows me to present this Baby as my Son. I am honored to give Him the name Jesus. I am humbled to raise Him as my own.

The prophecy we hear from Simeon in the Temple gives my heart grief. I know their lives will have sorrow and suffering. I sense that I will not be able to help them through the most difficult times. But as always, we trust in God...

Fourth Joyful Mystery - Lay the Roses

Mother Mary, I bind these pale blue roses with a petition for the grace of trust and humbly lay this bouquet at your feet.

Fifth Joyful Mystery - Finding of the Child Jesus in the Temple

Now his parents went to Jerusalem every year at the feast of the Passover. And when he was twelve years old, they went up according to custom; and when the feast was ended, as they were returning, the boy Jesus stayed behind in Jerusalem. His parents did not know it, but supposing him to be in the company they went a day's journey, and they sought him among their kinsfolk and acquaintances; and when they did not find him, they returned to Jerusalem, seeking him. After three days they found him in the temple, sitting among the teachers, listening to them and asking them questions; and all who heard him were amazed at his understanding and his answers. And when they saw him, they were astonished; and his mother said to him, "Son, why have you treated us so? Behold, your father and I have been looking for you anxiously." And he said to them, "How is it that you sought me? Did you not know that I must be in my Father's house?" And they did not understand the saying which he spoke to them. And he went down with them and came to Nazareth and was obedient to them; and his mother kept all these things in her heart.

And Jesus increased in wisdom and in stature, and in favor with God and man. ~Luke 2:41-52

I, Joseph, have the honor and privilege of being the father of God's Son. I am watching Jesus grow. I train Him in my trade. I am teaching Him our faith. We read the Holy Scriptures and the Jewish law. We pray together. "Hear, O Israel! The Lord is our God, the Lord alone! Therefore, you shall love the Lord, your God, with all your heart, and with all your soul, and with all your strength." We not only read and pray this, but we live it. Our discussions are helping Jesus to know and understand who He truly is and the mission He has. I see this grow in Him. It is not easy knowing what lies ahead for the Messiah. My heart aches for Jesus and Mary just as it burns with love for them...

Fifth Joyful Mystery - Lay the Roses

Mother Mary, I bind these pale blue roses with a petition for the grace of understanding and humbly lay this bouquet at your feet.

Day 16

First Sorrowful Mystery - Jesus' Agony in the Garden

I, Mary, pray as Jesus prays. My Son has His agony, and so do I, in my heart. I want to be there with Him, ministering to Him like the angel, wiping up His drops of sweat and blood. I know He has to suffer, yet I also know how much mankind is suffering and will continue to do so. I pray for my Son but also for you. I always pray for you. My sorrowful heart continues to suffer...

First Sorrowful Mystery - Lay the Roses

Mother Mary, I bind these violet roses with a petition for the grace of compassion and humbly lay this bouquet at your feet.

Second Sorrowful Mystery - Jesus is Scourged at the Pillar

The blows that Jesus experiences are terrible. I feel them in my body too. What mother wouldn't? I feel them very deeply in my heart as if my own heart is being tortured. But I know it is necessary. As the flesh is torn off my Son's body, my heart feels the same way...

Second Sorrowful Mystery - Lay the Roses

Mother Mary, I bind these violet roses with a petition for the grace of atonement and humbly lay this bouquet at your feet.

Third Sorrowful Mystery - Jesus is Crowned with Thorns

I have to watch my Son, our King being treated so violently, each insult, taunt, and slap. As the thorns are pressed into His head, they also pierce my heart. As His blood drips down His beautiful face, I can feel my heart leaking. God in His love continues to fill it, or I would not survive...

Third Sorrowful Mystery - Lay the Roses

Mother Mary, I bind these violet roses with a petition for the grace of strength and humbly lay this bouquet at your feet.

Fourth Sorrowful Mystery - Jesus Carries His Cross

My heart wants to help my Son, to carry the wood for Him. But this is not for me to do. So, I carry it silently, interiorly. This is my cross to bear, to see my Son suffer so and not be able to help Him physically. I feel the splinters of wood that break His skin. My suffering is helping Him by helping you. That is my role...

Fourth Sorrowful Mystery - Lay the Roses

Mother Mary, I bind these violet roses with a petition for the grace of perseverance and humbly lay this bouquet at your feet.

Fifth Sorrowful Mystery - The Crucifixion of our Lord and Savior Jesus Christ

The piercing of my Son's hands and feet by the nails almost brings me to my knees. Thankfully I have John's support, or I would not be able to bear it. I understand Simeon's prophecy in the Temple, for my heart and soul are pierced seeing my Son die like this on the cross. I pray for strength for us to endure, our Hearts united in pain and suffering, in sacrifice and offering. The thrust of the lance into my Son's Heart feels like it goes into my own as well...

Fifth Sorrowful Mystery - Lay the Roses

Mother Mary, I bind these violet roses with a petition for the grace of loyalty and humbly lay this bouquet at your feet.

Day 17

First Glorious Mystery - The Resurrection of Jesus

Before my Son's Body is resurrected, Jesus' soul joins ours in the realm of the dead. He descends there as our Savior, proclaiming the Good News. I, Joseph, and the others have been awaiting our entrance into heaven and into the vision of God. What a joy to have Jesus lead us there. From heaven I have a new ability to intercede. I am in the presence of the Father of Whom I had the privilege of being the representative on earth. My chaste heart beats with love for all of God's children.

First Glorious Mystery - Lay the Roses

Mother Mary, I bind these pure white roses with a petition for the grace of redemption and humbly lay this bouquet at your feet.

Second Glorious Mystery - The Ascension of Jesus into Heaven

At Jesus' ascension into heaven, I am once again reunited with my Son. My heart, which is set aflame with love for God, is rekindled at this reunion. I desire to intercede for you on earth as you carry on the work of Jesus, my adopted Son.

Second Glorious Mystery - Lay the Roses

Mother Mary, I bind these pure white roses with a petition for the grace of heavenly assistance and humbly lay this bouquet at your feet.

Third Glorious Mystery - The Descent of the Holy Spirit

From heaven, I am watching over Mary and the disciples as they pray in the upper room. I pray with them and for them. I witness

God's presence in the Holy Spirit descend upon them and give them power. I see this happening with you as well, when you receive the Sacraments and when you pray to God asking Him for His guidance and inspiration. You receive His Presence.

Third Glorious Mystery - Lay the Roses

Mother Mary, I bind these pure white roses with a petition for the grace of receiving God and humbly lay this bouquet at your feet.

Fourth Glorious Mystery - The Assumption of Mary into Heaven

Mary's assumption into heaven is joyous for me. I have great happiness at being in her presence again. We share a special love that is pure and strong. Our affection flows from our complete and perfect love that we have for God. This is the love that we gave to our Son and that we also give to the world.

Fourth Glorious Mystery - Lay the Roses

Mother Mary, I bind these pure white roses with a petition for the grace of love and humbly lay this bouquet at your feet.

Fifth Glorious Mystery - The Coronation of Mary as Queen of Heaven and Earth

This occasion is truly glorious. All of heaven rejoices as Mary is crowned its Queen. She and I have a special nobility given to us by God, through the line of David and through our Son, God's Son. This was hidden while we lived on earth, but God allows Mary's magnificent majesty to shine forth as is so fitting for her.

Fifth Glorious Mystery - Lay the Roses

Mother Mary, I bind these pure white roses with a petition for the grace of honor and humbly lay this bouquet at your feet.

Day 18

First Luminous Mystery - The Baptism of Jesus in the Jordan River

I, your Jesus, am here for you. My Heart is for you and for all humanity. It is the Heart of the Father, the Son, and the Holy Spirit. We manifest Ourselves to the world as the Most Holy Trinity to show Our Love to you, Our beloved. Let us together be recreated anew in the waters of baptism. Let us live the promises together. I am with you. I give Myself to you. Let today be a new beginning.

First Luminous Mystery - Lay the Roses

Mother Mary, I bind these orange roses with a petition for the grace of renewal and humbly lay this bouquet at your feet.

Second Luminous Mystery - The Wedding at Cana

I, Jesus, reveal Myself at Cana to show My Love for you. My Heart wants to provide for you. I come as the Bridegroom to cherish and care for you. This is how I love you, how I want to help you. I give you all you need, even more than you need. Mine is a Heart that knows only love and abundance.

Second Luminous Mystery - Lay the Roses

Mother Mary, I bind these orange roses with a petition for the grace of generosity and humbly lay this bouquet at your feet.

Third Luminous Mystery - The Proclamation of the Kingdom of God

My Heart wants your wholeness. Allow Me to heal you. I am the Divine Physician. My Heart wants you to know the Father and the

Spirit. Open yourself to your God; come to know God's love. Like a shepherd, I hold you, My little lamb, close to My Heart.

Third Luminous Mystery - Lay the Roses

Mother Mary, I bind these orange roses with a petition for the grace of healing and humbly lay this bouquet at your feet.

Fourth Luminous Mystery - The Transfiguration of Jesus

My Heart wants enlightenment. See the Light as it radiates forth from My Body. Let it permeate you and your heart. Feel the Light of My Love. Let it shine into your whole being: heart, mind, body, soul. Let it flow into your home and family.

Fourth Luminous Mystery - Lay the Roses

Mother Mary, I bind these orange roses with a petition for the grace of enlightenment and humbly lay this bouquet at your feet.

Fifth Luminous Mystery - The Institution of the Eucharist

My Eucharistic Heart feeds and nourishes. I desire to give you all that you require spiritually, physically, emotionally. I give My very Self. You have all you need in Me. You receive My whole being: Body, Blood, Soul, and Divinity. I want to heal and transform you. Allow Me. Be aware that you truly receive Me. Be open to My Love. It is My actual Heart that becomes a part of you. Let it give you My Life!

Fifth Luminous Mystery - Lay the Roses

Mother Mary, I bind these orange roses with a petition for the grace of sustenance and humbly lay this bouquet at your feet.

Day 19

First Sorrowful Mystery - Jesus' Agony in the Garden

My Sacred Heart is hurting, suffering for all humanity. So many people are far from God. If you could only know how much you are loved, if you could feel this Love. Yet still so many people refuse it, and turn away from Me, even while I long for you.

First Sorrowful Mystery - Lay the Roses

Mother Mary, I bind these blood red roses with a petition for the grace of receiving God's Love and humbly lay this bouquet at your feet.

Second Sorrowful Mystery - Jesus is Scourged at the Pillar

Just as My Heart suffers, so does My Body. My flesh is torn open in pain to repair the sins of the flesh of the world. I allow this because of My love for you. My Body is injured to heal yours.

Second Sorrowful Mystery - Lay the Roses

Mother Mary, I bind these blood red roses with a petition for the grace of healing and humbly lay this bouquet at your feet.

Third Sorrowful Mystery - Jesus is Crowned with Thorns

My Heart feels humanity's rejection of God. What great sorrow it causes Me. You may know how it feels to be unloved. I am not only unloved but disdained and despised by so many. But I do not want to force you to honor Me. I want it willingly.

Third Sorrowful Mystery - Lay the Roses

Mother Mary, I bind these blood red roses with a petition for the grace of honor and humbly lay this bouquet at your feet.

Fourth Sorrowful Mystery - Jesus Carries His Cross

My Body is weak. My Heart is weak. I have endured so much and lost so much blood. Yet, I continue on, for you. More drops of blood fall. They mark the path to My cross. Will you follow them?

Fourth Sorrowful Mystery - Lay the Roses

Mother Mary, I bind these blood red roses with a petition for the grace of endurance and humbly lay this bouquet at your feet.

Fifth Sorrowful Mystery - The Crucifixion and Death of our Lord Jesus Christ

My Heart gives everything for you. I stretch out my arms upon the cross. I open them wide waiting for your embrace. This is what I thirst for, your love. I give you Mine. Will you give Me yours?

Fifth Glorious Mystery - Lay the Roses

Mother Mary, I bind these blood red roses with a petition for the grace of love and humbly lay this bouquet at your feet.

Day 20

First Joyful Mystery - The Annunciation

My child, it is your Mother leading you to better understand my Immaculate Heart. The angel Gabriel called me "Full of Grace." This was a great gift from God. I did not earn this name on my own. God is perfectly holy, so I had to be holy also in order to be a proper dwelling place for His Son. My heart is Immaculate because my Son's heart is so pure. I am still humbled by this. My heart has always burned with love for God. With Jesus' Presence within me, this love grew in a way I had not known possible.

First Joyful Mystery - Lay the Roses

Mother Mary, I bind these pink roses with a petition for the grace of purity of heart and humbly lay this bouquet at your feet.

Second Joyful Mystery - The Visitation

Elizabeth called me "blessed among women." This blessedness comes from God continuing to pour His love into my heart and allowing me to share my heart with others. God's Presence continues to work, act, and perfect the soul in which He dwells. He gave me great love for all. My heart can't help but burst forth in praise of Him in my canticle. "The Almighty has done great things for me, and holy is His name."

Second Joyful Mystery - Lay the Roses

Mother Mary, I bind these pink roses with a petition for the grace of praise and humbly lay this bouquet at your feet.

Third Joyful Mystery - The Birth of Jesus

At the birth of my Son, the angel declared to the shepherds, "Behold, I proclaim to you good news of great joy that will be for all the people. For today in the city of David a savior has been born for you who is Messiah and Lord." This indeed was a great joy. My heart knew so much happiness and love. Just holding the infant Jesus in my arms was bliss. Here, I give Him to you now. Take Him in your arms. Let the joy flow into your heart too.

Third Joyful Mystery - Lay the Roses

Mother Mary, I bind these pink roses with a petition for the grace of joy and humbly lay this bouquet at your feet.

Fourth Joyful Mystery - The Presentation of the Baby Jesus in the Temple

When Joseph and I took the baby Jesus to the Temple, we marveled at Simeon's remarkable words. To me he said, "A sword will pierce through your own soul also, that thoughts out of many hearts may be revealed." Even though I knew there would be great suffering ahead, it was already taking place. My heart and soul are forever pierced by God, but it is pierced with Love. This allows the thoughts of your heart to come to me, so we can be united in our hearts and with my Son's Heart.

Fourth Joyful Mystery - Lay the Roses

Mother Mary, I bind these pink roses with a petition for the grace of unity and humbly lay this bouquet at your feet.

Fifth Joyful Mystery - The Finding of the Child Jesús in the Temple

There were many experiences in our lives that Joseph and I did not understand and that were difficult for us. When we found Jesus in the Temple after three days, I said to him, "Son, why have you done this to us? Your father and I have been looking for you with great anxiety." Being apart from Jesus for three days and not knowing how He was put a great strain on my heart. I know God had a reason for this. I know my Son was feeling the pull to His mission and that I had to be prepared. I kept many things in my heart and prayed with them, asking God to give me what I needed. My heart always trusts in Him.

Fifth Joyful Mystery - Lay the Roses

Mother Mary, I bind these pink roses with a petition for the grace of trust and humbly lay this bouquet at your feet.

Day 21

First Glorious Mystery - The Resurrection of Jesus

The Heart of the Father is loving. And this Love is made manifest in His Son, Jesus. In the Gospel of John, the apostle Philip said to Jesus, *"Master, show us the Father and that will be enough for us." Jesus said to him, "Have I been with you so long a time and you still do not know me, Philip? Whoever has seen me has seen the Father."* Jesus came to reveal to me the Father, who is Love.

God wants me to know that He loves me, not for what I do or do not do. He loves me just for who I am and for being me. I do not have to earn His love. It is unconditional and constant.

The first letter of Saint John tells me that God is love. *"We have come to know and to believe in the love God has for us. God is love, and whoever remains in love remains in God and God in him."* God would have sent His Son to die and rise for me even if I was the only person on earth.

I will ponder that unconditional love that You have for me, Father. A love so strong that You want to be united with me.

First Glorious Mystery - Lay the Roses

Mother Mary, I bind these golden yellow roses with a petition for the grace of love and humbly lay this bouquet at your feet.

Second Glorious Mystery - The Ascension of Jesus

The Heart of the Father disciplines. When He ascended into heaven it seemed that Jesus was taken away from the world. Sometimes I need to experience a type of loss to move on to what is next for me or to force me to grow and reach for God in a new way. I sometimes hold too tightly to certain things, therefore not realizing when there are better and more glorious opportunities awaiting. I may need to let go of an old way of thinking or living to move on to the next step that God has for me.

In the gospel of John, Jesus says, *"I am the true vine, and my Father is the vine grower. He takes away every branch in me that does not bear fruit and every one that does he prunes so that it bears more fruit...I am the vine, you are the branches. Whoever remains in me and I in him will bear much fruit, because without me you can do nothing."*

Father, I will let You show me what might need pruning. At the time it is happening, discipline feels like it hurts or is restrictive, but it actually prepares me to live more freely. Discipline means self-control.

The letter to the Hebrews states, *"At the time, all discipline seems a cause not for joy but for pain, yet later it brings the peaceful fruit of righteousness to those who are trained by it."*

Father, I know that You only do this for my good and my growth. And You love me perfectly, so You only want what is best for me. I will be Your disciple.

Second Glorious Mystery - Lay the Roses

Mother Mary, I bind these golden yellow roses with a petition for the grace of discipline and humbly lay this bouquet at your feet.

Third Glorious Mystery - The Descent of the Holy Spirit

The Heart of the Father is present to me. He is not a distant or absent Father but is very real and active in my life and wants me to be aware of that. He is concerned with every little detail and wants to share each moment with me. The Father wants to give Himself to me completely. When I ask Him, He pours Himself into me.

Sometimes I view God the Father as someone looking down on me and judging what I am doing. In reality, God is not just 'up there,' but He is 'in here.' He unites His Heart to mine and is present within. And He does not want me to fear, for He is with me, filling me with His Love.

"I command you: be strong and steadfast! Do not fear nor be dismayed, for the LORD, your God, is with you wherever you go." ~Joshua 1:9

God wants to pour Himself into me, flowing directly into my heart. He wants to place His Spirit within me. Saint Paul tells me in his letter to the Romans, *"The love of God has been poured out into our hearts through the holy Spirit that has been given to us."*

Father, You continue to give Yourself to me. I will try to be aware of the presence of God in my heart and feel Your love. If I am struggling with this, I will call out to You and ask You to give me more of Yourself.

Third Glorious Mystery - Lay the Roses

Mother Mary, I bind these golden yellow roses with a petition for the grace of God's presence and humbly lay this bouquet at your feet.

Fourth Glorious Mystery - The Assumption of Mary into Heaven

The Heart of the Father is protective. God takes care of those who are His. He shows me this in Mary, in keeping her hidden most of her life and bringing her to Him at the end of her time on earth. The book of Revelation tells me, *"The woman herself fled into the desert where she had a place prepared by God, that there she might be taken care of."*

He keeps me close too. I am the one who pushes away from Him at times, but He wants only to protect me like a good Father. I allow Him to be that shield around me, my shelter.

You are my shelter; you guard me from distress; with joyful shouts of deliverance you surround me. ~Psalm 32:7

Jesus assures me of God's protection in the gospel of John: *"My Father, who has given them to me, is greater than all, and no one can take them out of the Father's hand."* Father, I will see and feel Your protection around me. I know that it is there, for You are truly here with me.

Fourth Glorious Mystery - Lay the Roses

Mother Mary, I bind these golden yellow roses with a petition for the grace of care and humbly lay this bouquet at your feet.

Fifth Glorious Mystery - The Coronation of Mary

The Heart of the Father is generous. Being a good Father, God wishes to give me every good thing. And being God, He knows what is best for me. I may not receive the fullness of all God wants for me until I am in heaven, but He also gives me what I need here. Saint James tells me, *"All good giving and every perfect gift is from above, coming down from the Father of lights."*

The greatest gift is my adoption into God's family, so I can rightly call Him Father. In his first letter, Saint John says, *"See what love the Father has bestowed on us that we may be called the children of God. Yet so we are."*

I will truly see You as my Father Who loves me as Your Own beloved child. I receive the love You have for me that can never be taken away. You want to give me eternity with You in heaven. Father, I accept Your gifts.

Fifth Glorious Mystery - Lay the Roses

Mother Mary, I bind these golden yellow roses with a petition for the grace of generosity and humbly lay this bouquet at your feet.

Week 4

This week we will focus on how we can grow with the Church as the Church. The Catholic Church gives us the liturgical calendar as a beautiful way to order our lives and our worship around the life of Christ. There has been a tradition within the history of the Church of honoring each day of the week in a certain way. We still do this in part. Most of us know that Fridays are when we recall Jesus' passion and death, and Saturday is the day to honor Mary. But every day of the week has a particular devotion, and I will point out some of these.

During our prayer this week, we are going to look at what it means to follow Jesus. What does it look like to be a disciple and an apostle? We will do this by focusing on some of the other individuals present in the mysteries and how they learned to be followers of Christ or how they failed to let Jesus into their hearts.

Day 22

First Joyful Mystery - The Annunciation

Monday has been the day that the Church traditionally remembers the angels. Angels are spiritual beings that can appear to people in human form. They can be powerful guardians and helpers to us. We believe that each of us is protected by an angel.

The archangel Gabriel approaches Mary at God's command. He bows to one lower than himself in service to God and His plan. Some of the angels had rebelled against God and His plan of salvation, but Gabriel is faithful to God. He has been given this important task.

Do I choose to serve God in all things or am I sometimes in opposition? Am I willing to lower myself to serve God as told? Do I see all people worthy of dignity and respect, having been created in the image and likeness of God? Do I acknowledge the guardian angel that is present with me and ask my angel for help?

First Joyful Mystery - Lay the Roses

Mother Mary, I bind these pale blue roses with a petition for the grace of obedience to God and humbly lay this bouquet at your feet.

Second Joyful Mystery - The Visitation

Elizabeth is an example of a faithful woman. Her faith in God is rewarded. God allows her to have a child after being unable to conceive, after years of prayer and waiting. She is blessed by God. To help her with the difficulties of carrying a child in old age, God sends her help, the Mother of her Lord. Elizabeth is open to the Holy Spirit, realizing that she is blessed to be in the presence of Mary and Jesus. She was also given the honor of announcing the name of her child.

How faithful am I to God when I do not get what I want, when my ideas are different from God's? Do I continue to pray and trust in Him and His plan for me, whatever that may be? Do I rejoice in all that God sends my way?

Second Joyful Mystery - Lay the Roses

Mother Mary, I bind these pale blue roses with a petition for the grace of faithfulness and humbly lay this bouquet at your feet.

Third Joyful Mystery - The Birth of Jesus

Shepherds are some of the lowest people in society in Jesus' time. Living with animals makes them both physically and ritually unclean. But God comes for all. No one is left out. The shepherds are given a great gift to be the first to learn of the birth of the Savior and the first to see Him. They believe what they hear and rejoice at this announcement from God. They are welcomed by Mary and Joseph.

Do I believe God when He tells me the incredible or the unexpected? Do I hurry to see Him and to give Him my praise? Do I bow down in worship of Him even when He is present in a way that is not obvious, like in the Eucharist?

Third Joyful Mystery - Lay the Roses

Mother Mary, I bind these pale blue roses with a petition for the grace of belief and humbly lay this bouquet at your feet.

Fourth Joyful Mystery - The Presentation of Jesus in the Temple

Simeon is a man who is open to God. He has a close relationship with the Lord, so he is able to realize when God is speaking to him and accepts what he hears. Simeon follows the inspirations of the Holy Spirit to be in the temple and to recognize the Christ Child when He arrives. Simeon allows himself to be God's vessel. The Holy Spirit speaks a prophecy through him that is remembered throughout history. He lives to serve God and waits for God's promise to him to be fulfilled.

Am I open to the Holy Spirit? Do I spend time in prayer with God to develop a close relationship with Him so I can understand how He speaks in my life? Am I willing to wait for God's promises to me to be fulfilled?

Fourth Joyful Mystery - Lay the Roses

Mother Mary, I bind these pale blue roses with a petition for the grace of relationship with God and humbly lay this bouquet at your feet.

Fifth Joyful Mystery - The Finding of the Child Jesus in the Temple

Jesus is found in the midst of the teachers in the Temple. He is listening to them and asking questions. These elders in the Temple do not reject Jesus because He is still a boy. Even though they do not know Him, they allow this 12 year-old boy to be a part of their discussion. They are amazed at His understanding.

Am I open to Jesus in whatever unexpected ways He might come to me? Do I listen to Him? Do I respond to His questions? Do I allow myself to learn from Him?

Fifth Joyful Mystery - Lay the Roses

Mother Mary, I bind these pale blue roses with a petition for the grace of openness and humbly lay this bouquet at your feet.

Day 23

First Sorrowful Mystery - Jesus' Agony in the Garden

When He goes into the garden to pray, Jesus takes His three closest friends. He needs them with Him as He approaches His darkest hour. When they are supposed to be praying with Him, they fall asleep. Surely, they can see Jesus is in agony. He is suffering and sweating blood. Still, they can't stay awake with Him.

How often do I put my own lesser needs above someone who is obviously suffering more than I am? How often do I put myself and my wants before God? Am I willing to spend one hour in prayer with Him? Can I stay awake and alert to His needs in others?

First Sorrowful Mystery - Lay the Roses

Mother Mary, I bind these violet roses with a petition for the grace of prayer and humbly lay this bouquet at your feet.

Second Sorrowful Mystery - Jesus is Scourged at the Pillar

There are many onlookers in the crowd watching as Jesus is scourged. How do they feel? Are they there to gawk and laugh? Do they have a morbid curiosity? Are they frightened or sad for Jesus? What emotions stir in them at this sight?

How do I feel viewing this scene? Am I just there for the spectacle, or am I really concerned? Does my heart go out to Jesus? Am I able to help Him? Do I help Him in His suffering Body of the Church?

Second Sorrowful Mystery - Lay the Roses

Mother Mary, I bind these violet roses with a petition for the grace of compassion and humbly lay this bouquet at your feet.

Third Sorrowful Mystery - Jesus is Crowned with Thorns

I see the Jewish leaders present for Jesus' passion. Most of them have instigated this. Many do not believe Jesus is the Messiah. They think He is a blasphemer and false prophet. Do they feel satisfied at this sight, of Jesus being mocked as a king? What is their idea of a king? Do they really worship God as their King? Do I? Who do I say that Jesus is?

Third Sorrowful Mystery - Lay the Roses

Mother Mary, I bind these violet roses with a petition for the grace of worship of God and humbly lay this bouquet at your feet.

Fourth Sorrowful Mystery - Jesus Carries His Cross

While carrying the cross to His death, Jesus encounters women who are mourning for Him and lamenting. Why are they here? He addresses them as Daughters of Jerusalem, telling them not to weep for Him but for themselves. What does Jesus mean by this? How do they react to what Jesus says to them?

How do I respond to Jesus carrying His cross? Do I weep for Jesus? Do I weep for myself?

Fourth Sorrowful Mystery - Lay the Roses

Mother Mary, I bind these violet roses with a petition for the grace of sorrow for sins and humbly lay this bouquet at your feet.

Fifth Sorrowful Mystery - The Crucifixion and Death of Our Lord Jesus Christ

Some of Jesus' most faithful followers are the women who accompanied Him. Several are with Him at the cross as He is dying.

Am I strong enough to stand with Him and Mary at this horrible scene?

I think of the three Marys. One is quiet and often in the background yet there with them. Another is passionately faithful to Jesus, having been set free from her demons. His Mother is the perfect disciple, always saying yes to God. Which one am I most like? Have I been like all of them at different points in my life?

Fifth Sorrowful Mystery - Lay the Roses

Mother Mary, I bind these violet roses with a petition for the grace of faithfulness and humbly lay this bouquet at your feet.

Day 24

First Glorious Mystery - The Resurrection of Jesus

Peter has several encounters with the risen Christ. How does Peter feel during these? He had denied even knowing his Savior and his best friend. Yet, Jesus does not hold this against him. He makes an effort to reach out to Peter in love and healing.

Do I feel unwilling to approach Jesus, or do I let Him approach me when I need healing and reconciliation? Do I accept the great gift He offers me in the Sacrament of Reconciliation? Do I truly believe that God forgives me?

First Glorious Mystery - Lay the Roses

Mother Mary, I bind these pure white roses with a petition for the grace of reconciliation and humbly lay this bouquet at your feet.

Second Glorious Mystery - The Ascension of Jesus into Heaven

Peter watches as his Lord ascends into heaven, leaving Peter in charge of the Church. Peter is experiencing many emotions. Does he realize that this is the last time he will see Jesus? He is told he will receive power and will be Jesus' witness.

Do I believe that these words are meant for me also? Do I accept the responsibility that Jesus gives to me? Do I know that He will always be with me, even when I do not see or feel Him?

Second Glorious Mystery - Lay the Roses

Mother Mary, I bind these pure white roses with a petition for the grace of the power of God and humbly lay this bouquet at your feet.

Third Glorious Mystery - The Descent of the Holy Spirit

Peter and the other disciples return to Jerusalem and devote themselves to prayer. They pray for nine days while waiting for the Holy Spirit. Then they receive God's power and use it. Filled with the Holy Spirit, Peter goes out and preaches and converts 3,000 people in one day.

How dedicated am I to prayer? Am I willing to pray this long? Do I work with God's Presence within me? How bold am I in talking to others about Jesus?

Third Glorious Mystery - Lay the Roses

Mother Mary, I bind these pure white roses with a petition for the grace of courage and humbly lay this bouquet at your feet.

Fourth Glorious Mystery - The Assumption of Mary into Heaven

After Pentecost, Mary and the apostles build up the Church. They work together and help one another. John is obedient to Jesus in caring for Mary until her assumption.

How obedient am I to what God calls me to do? What part do I take in building up the Body of Christ? Do I care for the Church and for each member lovingly?

Fourth Glorious Mystery - Lay the Roses

Mother Mary, I bind these pure white roses with a petition for the grace of obedience and humbly lay this bouquet at your feet.

Fifth Glorious Mystery - The Coronation of Mary as Queen of Heaven and Earth

The Church is the Mystical Body of Christ. Do I remember that I am a part of the Church militant because I am struggling against the world, the flesh, and the devil? Do I actively fight these things? Do I remember the Church suffering and pray for the souls in purgatory? Am I always keeping in mind my destination, my ultimate goal, which is heaven with the Church triumphant? Do I strive to live my life in light of eternity, trying to see all things as God sees them? When I look back at my life from heaven, am I going to be satisfied with how I lived?

Fifth Glorious Mystery - Lay the Roses

Mother Mary, I bind these pure white roses with a petition for the grace of focusing on eternity and humbly lay this bouquet at your feet.

Day 25

First Luminous Mystery - Jesus' Baptism in the Jordan River

John the Baptist has an essential part in God's plan of salvation, and he accepts his role. John does not try to be any more or less than what God wants him to be, the person to announce the coming of the Savior. Some think that he is the Messiah, but John points the way to the actual Lamb of God and acknowledges that "He must increase while I must decrease."

Am I willing to let Jesus, or even others increase as I decrease, or do I want to be the one to be noticed? Do I accept and live out my part of God's plan? Do I even know my role? Do I want to know?

First Luminous Mystery - Lay the Roses

Mother Mary, I bind these orange roses with a petition for the grace of cooperation and humbly lay this bouquet at your feet.

Second Luminous Mystery - The Wedding at Cana

Jesus and His disciples are invited to the wedding. The miracle that Jesus performs at Cana is the first of His signs and reveals His glory. With this, the disciples begin to believe in Him. All that the disciples do is show up at the wedding. They accept the invitation.

How often am I invited but do not bother to attend to what God is doing in my life? Am I aware of the miracles that He is performing? Sometimes they are large and sometimes small. Am I watching for them? Am I present to God in my life and to the people He places there?

Second Luminous Mystery - Lay the Roses

Mother Mary, I bind these orange roses with a petition for the grace of being present and humbly lay this bouquet at your feet.

Third Luminous Mystery - The Proclamation of the Kingdom of God

Many people come to see Jesus and to hear Him speak. They are here for different reasons - curiosity, to learn, to be healed, to see a miracle, to be fed. Some have to make an effort to see Him, even following Him to remote places. And Jesus always makes Himself available.

How much effort do I put into my relationship with the Lord and being with Him? Do I follow Him if necessary? When I do show up, why am I there? Do I expect to get something? Do I have my own agenda or expectation, or do I let God decide what is best? Do I pray for my will or God's? Do I go to Mass to give God the worship that is due to Him or just to get something for myself?

Third Luminous Mystery - Lay the Roses

Mother Mary, I bind these orange roses with a petition for the grace of receptivity and humbly lay this bouquet at your feet.

Fourth Luminous Mystery - The Transfiguration of Jesus

Jesus leads Peter, James, and John up the mountain to pray. He does not send them by themselves but shows them the way. They follow not knowing what to expect, and they are shown a glorious sight.

Am I willing to follow Jesus even when the way is difficult? Do I take the time to really see Jesus in all His glory? Do I worship Him as God, or do I get distracted and start making my own plans (like

Peter's idea to build tents)? Do I let encounters with Jesus strengthen me?

Fourth Luminous Mystery - Lay the Roses

Mother Mary, I bind these orange roses with a petition for the grace of following God and humbly lay this bouquet at your feet.

Fifth Luminous Mystery - The Institution of the Eucharist

Jesus shares a very special meal with His apostles at the Last Supper. They are probably expecting a regular Passover, but this is a new Passover. Do the apostles realize the sacredness of this event?

Do I see Holy Thursday and Good Friday just as formalities? Is the Mass just another requirement I have to do on Sunday? Do I simply go to church, or do I pray the Mass, realizing that it is a re-presentation of Jesus' sacrifice and that I am actually there with Him? Am I as reverent as I should be?

Fifth Luminous Mystery - Lay the Roses

Mother Mary, I bind these orange roses with a petition for the grace of sacredness and humbly lay this bouquet at your feet.

Day 26

First Sorrowful Mystery - Jesus' Agony in the Garden

Jesus' time of praying in the garden of Gethsemane ends with the arrival of Judas, His betrayer. Jesus tells the others that the hour has come. Judas is here with soldiers, temple guards of the chief priest, and some of the elders. He identifies Jesus with a kiss. Judas allows himself to be lured by greed and other sinful thoughts and behaviors that eventually lead him to this point. If he had truly let Jesus into his heart, would he have done this?

Do I ever betray Jesus? Do I say that I am His and then turn my back on Him, or worse? Do I allow Jesus into my heart so He can get rid of any sinful tendencies and guide me only toward love?

First Sorrowful Mystery - Lay the Roses

Mother Mary, I bind these blood red roses with a petition for the grace of restoration and humbly lay this bouquet at your feet.

Second Sorrowful Mystery - Jesus is Scourged at the Pillar

The scourging that Jesus endures is harsh. These are trained soldiers and guards who do not show mercy. Yet, how can they administer such a cruel whipping? What is in their hearts? They did not begin life this way. Hate and evil tend to build over time, little by little. The enemy works his way into the heart. Even now in this scourging, Jesus still loves them.

What do I do with each negative thing that tries to creep into my life, every little bad habit or sin? Do I say it does not matter, it is just a small thing and isn't hurting anyone? Or do I try to stop it right away, so it does not grow, like it did with these men?

Second Sorrowful Mystery - Lay the Roses

Mother Mary, I bind these blood red roses with a petition for the grace of repentance and humbly lay this bouquet at your feet.

Third Sorrowful Mystery - Jesus is Crowned with Thorns

Once again, the guards mistreat Jesus, mocking Him, spitting on Him, forcing the thorns upon His head and hitting them into His skull. It is hard to imagine treating another human in this way, let alone our God. Do they not see Him as a person?

Do I see others in the way that I should, the way that God does? Do I treat God the way that He deserves, as my King?

Third Sorrowful Mystery - Lay the Roses

Mother Mary, I bind these blood red roses with a petition for the grace of respect and humbly lay this bouquet at your feet.

Fourth Sorrowful Mystery - Jesus Carries His Cross

Jesus is so weak that the guards fear He will die before He reaches the place of execution. Simon the Cyrenian, is taken from the crowd to carry the cross for Jesus. I wonder how Simon feels about this. Is he surprised, reluctant but afraid of the guards, and possibly annoyed at being rendered ritually unclean? He seems to help only because he is forced. Does this encounter with Jesus change him?

Do I only help when I am coerced? When can I be like Simon and help someone else? Do I allow others to be like Simon for me when I need it?

Fourth Sorrowful Mystery - Lay the Roses

Mother Mary, I bind these blood red roses with a petition for the grace of helpfulness and humbly lay this bouquet at your feet.

Fifth Sorrowful Mystery - The Crucifixion and Death of Our Lord Jesus Christ

John is the beloved, faithful disciple who remains at the cross with Our Lady and a few of the women. While the others have denied Jesus and run away from Him, John stays to endure the whole experience of Jesus' crucifixion.

Am I faithful to Jesus and Mary? Do I remain with them even when things are difficult or seemingly hopeless? How can I let God strengthen me and my faith to endure even the most difficult situations?

Fifth Sorrowful Mystery - Lay the Roses

Mother Mary, I bind these blood red roses with a petition for the grace of faithfulness and humbly lay this bouquet at your feet.

Day 27

First Joyful Mystery - The Annunciation

Tradition reveals that Mary's parents are Saints Anne and Joachim. It is believed they were infertile for many years. God gives them an immaculate child after Joachim's 40 days of prayer and fasting. They stay faithful to God despite their disappointment. They take their desire for a child to God in prayer. It is also believed that Mary is consecrated to God and goes to live in the temple at age three. God blesses them with a child, whom they give back to Him.

Do I accept God's plans for my life? Do I complain when things do not go according to what I would like, or do I take this to prayer? Do I thank God accordingly for hearing my prayers? How can I be more like Anne and Joachim?

First Joyful Mystery - Lay the Roses

Mother Mary, I bind these pale pink roses with a petition for the grace of perseverance in prayer and humbly lay this bouquet at your feet.

Second Joyful Mystery - The Visitation

Zechariah, the husband of Elizabeth, is visited by the angel Gabriel who announces the birth of his son. But Zechariah doubts the angel's words and experiences the consequence of his lack of faith.

Do I doubt God's word to me? Am I willing to humble myself when I know that I am wrong? Are there times when I just need to be quiet and listen to God and let His plan unfold?

Second Joyful Mystery - Lay the Roses

Mother Mary, I bind these pale pink roses with a petition for the grace of humility and humbly lay this bouquet at your feet.

Third Joyful Mystery - The Birth of Jesus

The Magi see the sign that God places in the sky indicating the birth of His Son. God puts the star there for all to see to show that He came for all. The Magi do not view this as just a beautiful sight and rare phenomenon. But they choose to see where God is leading them, even on a long journey to a foreign land. They are guided by God's sign and listen to the angel when returning home.

Do I notice the beautiful and extraordinary signs that God places in my life? Do I ask God what He wants me to know from them and where they will lead me? Do I then listen to Him and follow the path that He sets out for me?

Third Joyful Mystery - Lay the Roses

Mother Mary, I bind these pale pink roses with a petition for the grace of awareness and humbly lay this bouquet at your feet.

Fourth Joyful Mystery - The Presentation in the Temple

Anna is in the Temple when Mary and Joseph arrive with the Child Jesus. A widow for many years, she is devout and faithful. She never leaves the Temple, but worships night and day with fasting and prayer. God rewards her faithfulness with being able to see the Messiah. She thanks God for this opportunity and speaks to others about Jesus.

How faithful am I to God in prayer? Do I put God first in my life? Do I remember to thank Him when He shows me great kindness? Do I speak eagerly to others about Jesus?

Fourth Joyful Mystery - Lay the Roses

Mother Mary, I bind these pale pink roses with a petition for the grace of faithfulness and humbly lay this bouquet at your feet.

Fifth Joyful Mystery - The Finding of Jesus in the Temple

The Holy Family goes to Jerusalem for the feast of Passover every year. They travel in a caravan with their relatives and acquaintances from Nazareth. They make this journey together, sharing in the celebration and the joys. They also share in the sorrow of the loss of the Child Jesus.

Do I consider my faith to be just between me and God, or am I willing to share it with others, especially those closest to me? Being Christian means being in community. How can my loved ones and I support one another on our spiritual journey? How can I truly be a part of my community in a more Christian manner?

Fifth Joyful Mystery - Lay the Roses

Mother Mary, I bind these pale pink roses with a petition for the grace of accompaniment and humbly lay this bouquet at your feet.

Week 5

We are halfway through the rosary novena! That means today we begin praying in thanksgiving for Mary's intercession for our needs, confident that she is helping us according to God's most holy will, even if we do not see an answer to our prayers yet.

Our focus this week will be on quiet and stillness. We will strive to find some peaceful moments and spend them with God, listening to Him. God sees how busy many of us are. Our lives may seem hectic.

Please try to make the time to pray. Our need for quiet is very real. It is essential to our well-being and our relationship with God. He wants to provide us with a chance to get away from the world and be with Him so He can renew us.

While meditating on the mysteries, we are going to search for those quiet moments and sit with them. We will ponder what God is doing, what we can learn, and what He is trying to tell us. Remember, God is ever-present and available in every moment. Seek Him in the silence. That is where we are most able to hear Him. God speaks in the silence!

Place yourself there in a quiet, contemplative way, as Mary would, reflecting in your heart. Experience the peace and the stillness that your mind and body need.

Come, pray in the quiet...

Day 28

First Glorious Mystery - The Resurrection of Jesus

I am outside the tomb on that first Easter morning. Jesus has already risen. The tomb is open with the stone rolled away. Mary Magdalene and the women have been here. Peter and John have come and gone as well. I sit *in the stillness* contemplating what has happened.

First Glorious Mystery - Lay the Roses

Mother Mary, I bind these golden yellow roses with a petition for the grace of peace and humbly lay this bouquet at your feet.

Second Glorious Mystery - The Ascension of Jesus

I am with the crowd that has just arrived at the top of the mountain with Jesus. Others are still coming. After the walk, I want a little rest. I go off a short distance to a quiet place by myself, wondering why Jesus has led us here. I ponder and pray.

Second Glorious Mystery - Lay the Roses

Mother Mary, I bind these golden yellow roses with a petition for the grace of reflection and humbly lay this bouquet at your feet.

Third Glorious Mystery - The Descent of the Holy Spirit

I have been praying with the disciples for days. I am tired and not sure what to expect. I want some time to myself. I find a quiet corner, away from everyone else. I sit down and contemplate all that has happened so far. I wait on God to speak and act.

Third Glorious Mystery - Lay the Roses

Mother Mary, I bind these golden yellow roses with a petition for the grace of patience and humbly lay this bouquet at your feet.

Fourth Glorious Mystery - The Assumption of Mary

The apostles have gone to different places to preach to the world about Jesus. Mary is living with John. I see them in their humble home, Mary close to the end of her life. They are both at peace. I am able to observe this quiet moment with them and how they are content with where God has each of them in life at this moment. I pray with that feeling and ask for the same.

Fourth Glorious Mystery - Lay the Roses

Mother Mary, I bind these golden yellow roses with a petition for the grace of contentment and humbly lay this bouquet at your feet.

Fifth Glorious Mystery - The Coronation of Mary

I have been given a glimpse of heaven. Mary is there with Joseph and the other saints and the angels. I see some of my loved ones who have already passed away. I notice their happiness. It fills me with peace. I rest in that serenity.

Fifth Glorious Mystery - Lay the Roses

Mother Mary, I bind these golden yellow roses with a petition for the grace of serenity and humbly lay this bouquet at your feet.

Day 29

First Joyful Mystery - The Annunciation

I am in the room with Mary before the angel arrives. There is a quietness in Mary's being, a sense of contentedness. When the angel appears, a new feeling arrives, a sense of wonder. As the Holy Spirit overshadows Mary, the atmosphere changes again. An aura of glory fills not only her but the entire space. I feel it and pray with that sensation. I treasure these occasions that God shares with me and know that since He is in everything, these moments are always available.

First Joyful Mystery - Lay the Roses

Mother Mary, I bind these pale blue roses with a petition for the grace of a sense of the divine and humbly lay this bouquet at your feet.

Second Joyful Mystery - The Visitation

Mary is on her journey to visit Elizabeth. It takes several days. I see her in those quiet moments in the evening before she sleeps. She spends time in prayer with the Father but also speaking to God as the infant in her womb. She talks to the Child within her. I hear her softly singing to Him.

Second Joyful Mystery - Lay the Roses

Mother Mary, I bind these pale blue roses with a petition for the grace of time with God and humbly lay this bouquet at your feet.

Third Joyful Mystery - The Birth of Jesus

I picture the scene in the stable in Bethlehem. Mary and Joseph have not yet arrived. This is what they will come to after their long journey. Many people would notice the smell and the filth. Mary and Joseph will see the warmth on the cold night, the stillness of the reposing animals, the comfort of a place to rest. I view the surroundings in the way they will, and it gives me comfort too.

Third Joyful Mystery - Lay the Roses

Mother Mary, I bind these pale blue roses with a petition for the grace of optimism and humbly lay this bouquet at your feet.

Fourth Joyful Mystery - The Presentation of the Baby Jesus in the Temple

I watch Joseph and Mary with the baby Jesus as they enter the Temple. The outside was noisy and busy. Inside the Temple there is an air of peacefulness. It is quieter, and the Holy Family relishes being in this holy place, where they feel at home. Mary pulls the infant closer to her as she softly hums to Him.

Fourth Joyful Mystery - Lay the Roses

Mother Mary, I bind these pale blue roses with a petition for the grace of peacefulness and humbly lay this bouquet at your feet.

Fifth Joyful Mystery - The Finding of the Child Jesus in the Temple

Joseph and Mary have been searching for their Child. They have not yet found Him. It is evening and they must stop and rest for the night. Their hearts are heavy. I watch them in their quiet time praying together. I pray too.

Fifth Joyful Mystery - Lay the Roses

Mother Mary, I bind these pale blue roses with a petition for the grace of resting in God and humbly lay this bouquet at your feet.

Day 30

First Sorrowful Mystery - The Agony of Jesus in the Garden

And to strengthen him an angel from heaven appeared to him. ~Luke 22:43

I am watching Jesus in the garden. I see the angel come to minister to Him. I feel like I am invading an intimate moment as I see the angel comfort my Lord, wiping the sweat from His face. The care that the angel takes with the Precious Blood of Jesus is remarkable. The angel reverences every drop.

First Sorrowful Mystery - Lay the Roses

Mother Mary, I bind these violet roses with a petition for the grace of giving comfort and humbly lay this bouquet at your feet.

Second Sorrowful Mystery - Jesus is Scourged at the Pillar

While he was still seated on the bench, his wife sent him a message, "Have nothing to do with that righteous man. I suffered much in a dream today because of him." ~Matthew 27:19

Pontius Pilate is unsure of what to do with Jesus. I can see his wife pacing in the background, worrying. I am praying for Pilate to make the right decision, even though I know how he will respond. Jesus waits for His death sentence, His body already wounded. I wait and pray silently.

Second Sorrowful Mystery - Lay the Roses

Mother Mary, I bind these violet roses with a petition for the grace of listening and humbly lay this bouquet at your feet.

Third Sorrowful Mystery - Jesus is Crowned with Thorns

And when they had mocked him, they stripped him of the purple cloak, dressed him in his own clothes, and led him out to crucify him. ~Mark 15:20

The purple cloak has been removed from my Lord and left in a heap on the ground. No one wants to touch it, covered in blood, sweat, dirt, and spittle. I look at it as Jesus is being led off. I stay behind, away from the jeering crowd and noise. I think about my King whom they do not recognize.

Third Sorrowful Mystery - Lay the Roses

Mother Mary, I bind these violet roses with a petition for the grace of honor and humbly lay this bouquet at your feet.

Fourth Sorrowful Mystery - Jesus Carries His Cross

Now two others, both criminals, were led away with him to be executed. ~Luke 23:32

Jesus is being led out of the city just like a criminal. The crowd is pressing around. I move back. I do not like being jostled about in this unusual mob of people. I do not want to be a part of this. I walk along, away from the others, praying and trying to understand.

Fourth Sorrowful Mystery - Lay the Roses

Mother Mary, I bind these violet roses with a petition for the grace of detachment from the world and humbly lay this bouquet at your feet.

Fifth Sorrowful Mystery - The Crucifixion and Death of our Lord Jesus Christ

At noon darkness came over the whole land until three in the afternoon. ~Mark 15:33

The darkness over the land reflects the blackness of the evil that is here and the denseness within hearts that are obscured from God. I hide in these shadows to keep from seeing what I do not want to see. But it forces me to look within. God gives this moment to reflect on what we have done to His Son and what we are doing to ourselves.

Fifth Sorrowful Mystery - Lay the Roses

Mother Mary, I bind these violet roses with a petition for the grace of introspection and humbly lay this bouquet at your feet.

Day 31

First Glorious Mystery - The Resurrection of Jesus

Jesus is alive! He has shown himself to many people. I am alone in the room where He has appeared to the apostles. The others are gone now. Jesus has just been here even though the doors were locked. He showed Thomas the holes in His body. I am sitting here by myself amazed, thinking about what they just experienced.

First Glorious Mystery - Lay the Roses

Mother Mary, I bind these pure white roses with a petition for the grace of belief and humbly lay this bouquet at your feet.

Second Glorious Mystery - The Ascension of Jesus into Heaven

We witnessed Jesus ascending from the earth into heaven. It was a glorious sight. The others have begun to head back down the mountain. I am sitting on the ground remembering. I saw Him go up into the clouds. I saw the two men dressed in white garments. Were they angels? I ponder all of this in my quiet time alone.

Second Glorious Mystery - Lay the Roses

Mother Mary, I bind these pure white roses with a petition for the grace of awe of God and humbly lay this bouquet at your feet.

Third Glorious Mystery - The Descent of the Holy Spirit

I am sitting in the upper room after the Holy Spirit's descent. The others have gone to proclaim the Good News. I want to take a quiet moment to praise and thank God for what He has done before going out myself to share this.

Third Glorious Mystery - Lay the Roses

Mother Mary, I bind these pure white roses with a petition for the grace of gratitude and humbly lay this bouquet at your feet.

Fourth Glorious Mystery - The Assumption of Mary into Heaven

Mary has left us. She is now with God in heaven. I am happy for her yet a bit sad for myself. Still, my role here in the Church continues. Mary wants us to persist in telling others about her Son. I spend some quiet time thinking about her gentle ways and of how she shared Jesus with us.

Fourth Glorious Mystery - Lay the Roses

Mother Mary, I bind these pure white roses with a petition for the grace of evangelization and humbly lay this bouquet at your feet.

Fifth Glorious Mystery - The Coronation of Mary as Queen of Heaven and Earth

It is a source of comfort to me knowing that Mary and the rest of the Church triumphant are in heaven praying for me. I draw strength from that knowledge that I have help here in all that I do. I am never on my own. I rest in that peace of mind.

Fifth Glorious Mystery - Lay the Roses

Mother Mary, I bind these pure white roses with a petition for the grace of intercession and humbly lay this bouquet at your feet.

Day 32

First Luminous Mystery - The Baptism of Jesus

Then Jesus was led by the Spirit into the desert. ~Matthew 4:1

After His baptism in the Jordan River, Jesus is led *by the Holy Spirit* into the wilderness where He undergoes fasting and temptation. I see Him in that wild land with nothing to eat. He relies on the strength that He receives from His Father. I pray with Him in the quiet.

First Luminous Mystery - Lay the Roses

Mother Mary, I bind these orange roses with a petition for the grace of reliance on God and humbly lay this bouquet at your feet.

Second Luminous Mystery - The Wedding at Cana

Jesus told them, "Fill the jars with water." So, they filled them to the brim. ~John 2:7

The wedding feast has ended, and the people have returned to their own homes. The servants are cleaning up from the celebration. They are still in awe of the miracle that has happened. They truly know what has occurred, for they had a part to play in it. There was so much wine, and there is still some left in the bottom of the jars that they had filled with water. I marvel with them during this fading evening. I remember and ponder the wonder and the significance of Jesus' act.

Second Luminous Mystery - Lay the Roses

Mother Mary, I bind these orange roses with a petition for the grace of recognizing the miraculous and humbly lay this bouquet at your feet.

Third Luminous Mystery - The Proclamation of the Kingdom of God

When they had had their fill, he said to his disciples, "Gather the fragments left over, so that nothing will be wasted." ~John 6:12

I am sitting on the hill finishing my bits of fish and bread as I watch the disciples of Jesus cleaning up. I take a moment to ponder what has just happened. I saw the original number of fish and loaves, but this is staggering. How has Jesus done this and what is the meaning? I sit alone to reflect on this.

Third Luminous Mystery - Lay the Roses

Mother Mary, I bind these orange roses with a petition for the grace of wonder and humbly lay this bouquet at your feet.

Fourth Luminous Mystery - The Transfiguration

They fell silent and did not at that time tell anyone what they had seen. ~Luke 9:36

I see Jesus descending the mountain with Peter, James, and John. They are walking in silence. Even Peter is unusually quiet. They are pondering the sight that they beheld at the top, marveling at what it means. I look up and wonder what they experienced.

Fourth Luminous Mystery - Lay the Roses

Mother Mary, I bind these orange roses with a petition for the grace of contemplation and humbly lay this bouquet at your feet.

Fifth Luminous Mystery - The Institution of the Eucharist

So, he took the morsel and left at once. And it was night. ~John 13:30

I see Judas present at the Last Supper. It is apparent, the turmoil within him. The other apostles are reclining at the table, relaxed and enjoying the time with Jesus. I feel an ache in my heart for the peace that Judas lacks. After he leaves, I take a moment to think about these things during this quiet time after the meal. Jesus seems to be pondering things as well.

Fifth Luminous Mystery - Lay the Roses

Mother Mary, I bind these orange roses with a petition for the grace of repentance and humbly lay this bouquet at your feet.

Day 33

First Sorrowful Mystery - The Agony of Jesus in the Garden

Jesus is praying in the garden. I am trying to pray too. I see the anxiety on His face. The drops of His sweat turn to blood. I see one drop fall onto a rock. It sits there in a small glistening puddle, seeming to quiver and shimmer. I reflect on the power in the one small drop of my Lord's blood!

First Sorrowful Mystery - Lay the Roses

Mother Mary, I bind these blood red roses with a petition for the grace of power of God and humbly lay this bouquet at your feet.

Second Sorrowful Mystery - Jesus is Scourged at the Pillar

I peek from behind a pillar to view Jesus as He is brutally flogged. As the whips hit His body, His blood is splattered in different directions. I watch as a drop of blood lands on one of the men doing the scourging. That blood has the ability to heal, to convert, to give new life. Does Jesus' Precious Blood affect this man, or is he so hardened in his heart that it does not alter him in any way? How does a drop of Jesus' blood change me?

Second Sorrowful Mystery - Lay the Roses

Mother Mary, I bind these blood red roses with a petition for the grace of renewal and humbly lay this bouquet at your feet.

Third Sorrowful Mystery - Jesus is Crowned with Thorns

I try to stay separated from the crowd as Jesus is mocked as king. When the crown of thorns is forced onto His head, the blood runs down His face and into His eyes. I wonder what Jesus sees and how the world looks to Him through the red tint of His own blood.

Third Sorrowful Mystery - Lay the Roses

Mother Mary, I bind these blood red roses with a petition for the grace of seeing as God sees and humbly lay this bouquet at your feet.

Fourth Sorrowful Mystery - Jesus Carries His Cross

I try to hide while still watching Jesus make His way through the narrow streets. He seems so tired and the cross so heavy. The blood continues to seep from His body, washing away my sins, soaking the wood that He carries. Drops of blood fall to the ground. What happens to those? I think of God telling Cain that Abel's blood cries out to Him from the ground. Is Jesus' blood crying out? Maybe if I am quiet, I will hear it. What does it say?

Fourth Sorrowful Mystery - Lay the Roses

Mother Mary, I bind these blood red roses with a petition for the grace of righteousness and humbly lay this bouquet at your feet.

Fifth Sorrowful Mystery - The Crucifixion and Death of our Lord Jesus Christ

I stay as far away from the crucifixion scene as I can and still see Jesus. His life is being poured out with His blood. It runs down the wood and stains the ground. His life for my life. I close my eyes and silently thank Him for His sacrifice as I imagine His blood and mercy washing over me.

Fifth Sorrowful Mystery - Lay the Roses

Mother Mary, I bind these blood red roses with a petition for the grace of new life and humbly lay this bouquet at your feet.

Day 34

First Joyful Mystery - The Annunciation

Mary said, "Behold, I am the handmaid of the Lord. May it be done to me according to your word." Then the angel departed from her. ~Luke 1:38

I see Mary after the angel has gone. Mary is left to continue with her life. She does it carrying God with her. She takes a few moments to praise and thank God for what He has just done for her. I see her connection with our Lord. I strive for that connection too.

First Joyful Mystery - Lay the Roses

Mother Mary, I bind these pale pink roses with a petition for the grace of connection with God in prayer and humbly lay this bouquet at your feet.

Second Joyful Mystery - The Visitation

"Mary remained with her about three months." ~Luke 1:56

Mary stays in the home of Elizabeth and Zechariah for several months. I see her there, a quiet, peaceful presence. Her influence on them in her own gentle way is subtle yet deep. Carrying Jesus with her during the assistance she offers the family has a profound impact on them in ways they do not even realize.

Second Joyful Mystery - Lay the Roses

Mother Mary, I bind these pale pink roses with a petition for the grace of gentleness and humbly lay this bouquet at your feet.

Third Joyful Mystery - The Birth of Jesus

"We saw his star at its rising and have come to do him homage." ~Matthew 2:2

I watch Mary and Joseph after the birth of Jesus. It is just the three of them, the parents adoring the Holy Child. They look out at the night sky on this holiest of nights. The sky is clear and there are many stars. One in particular shines brighter than all the others, sending its light directly down on them. The night is still and quiet except for the sound of angels singing over the nearby hills. Together we marvel at God's goodness.

Third Joyful Mystery - Lay the Roses

Mother Mary, I bind these pale pink roses with a petition for the grace of giving glory to God and humbly lay this bouquet at your feet.

Fourth Joyful Mystery - The Presentation in the Temple

"She never left the temple, but worshiped night and day with fasting and prayer." ~Luke 2:37

I am in the temple. It is very quiet, not many are here. There is an elderly woman named Anna praying alone. She is off to one side. I am at the other. Our prayers are both lifted up to the one true God, and we know He hears them. The Holy Family has gone. Anna seems quite content and fulfilled. Her prayers are of praise and gratitude. God has been good to her. He has been good to me too.

Fourth Joyful Mystery - Lay the Roses

Mother Mary, I bind these pale pink roses with a petition for the grace of gratitude and humbly lay this bouquet at your feet.

Fifth Joyful Mystery - The Finding in the Temple

He went down with them and came to Nazareth and was obedient to them; and his mother kept all these things in her heart. ~Luke 2:51

The Holy Family travels home to Nazareth together, the three of them. They are mostly quiet as they journey. The parents are pondering the events of the past few days. They do not fully understand. They ask God for guidance. Yet they are grateful to have their Son with them. Their hearts have been touched in many different ways, and they share this with God, each in their own manner.

Fifth Joyful Mystery - Lay the Roses

Mother Mary, I bind these pale pink roses with a petition for the grace of guidance from God and humbly lay this bouquet at your feet.

Week 6

I feel that in the meditations, God is meeting us where we are at the moment, but He is always preparing us for what is coming next. In working to calm the mind and put aside the distractions, we can become aware of God's presence. Let's keep disciplining ourselves to find the quiet. We need God, and prayer forms our relationship with Him. No matter where we are in our spiritual journey, we can always grow more and become closer to Him. He continually calls us to that.

We practiced last week how to still ourselves and find those quiet spaces in which to pray. We are going to continue with that by leaving the outside world behind and trying to remove obstacles to our stillness. This will help us to sense God's loving presence and to hear Him. *"Be still and know that I am God." Psalm 46:11.* You will also notice some repetition in the reflections as you saw in week 2.

God wants to continue to help us draw near to Him. He desires us to encounter Him in a new way. The most profound way to do that is to find Him within ourselves. God is knocking at that door of the inner room of our hearts. Let's be open to Him and all the graces He wishes to infuse in us. Trust Him and be ready to receive what He wants to give. Listen to Him call you by name. What does He say? Look into His eyes and see His love for you on His face.

Come, let us pray…

Day 35

First Glorious Mystery - The Resurrection of Jesus

I am walking along the road alone, confused and thinking God is gone, that He is dead. Someone approaches me from behind, hurrying to catch up with me. I hear my name and turn to see Him. He inquires about me, genuinely concerned. He accompanies me, looks at me with love, telling me what I need to hear. I listen to Him and learn, my heart burning within me.

First Glorious Mystery - Lay the Roses

Mother Mary, I bind these golden yellow roses with a petition for the grace of understanding and humbly lay this bouquet at your feet.

Second Glorious Mystery - The Ascension of Jesus into Heaven

I stand on the top of the mountain looking out and waiting. Jesus approaches me and calls to me by my name. I turn to face Him. As I look at Him, He sees my concern. He reminds me that He is always with me "in here" and touches my forehead. "I am also here," and He touches my heart. As He looks at me, He communicates the presence of His burning love to me.

Second Glorious Mystery - Lay the Roses

Mother Mary, I bind these golden yellow roses with a petition for the grace of love and humbly lay this bouquet at your feet.

Third Glorious Mystery - The Descent of the Holy Spirit

I am alone in the upper room. I have been praying. I look out the window at the mountain where I last saw Jesus, where He touched me. I experience that burning sensation again. This time it comes not only from inside but also from around me. I feel the air swirl and the rumbling of the walls. I sense the heat as God comes closer to me.

Third Glorious Mystery - Lay the Roses

Mother Mary, I bind these golden yellow roses with a petition for the grace of openness to God and humbly lay this bouquet at your feet.

Fourth Glorious Mystery - The Assumption of Mary into Heaven

I do not really know what the end of your life was like, dear Mother. You were free from all sin, perfect in every way. You would not have experienced death in a painful or fearful way. It would have been more like a gentle transition from one state of existence to another. One moment you were here, then as God called, you were fully with Him, present with Him in all His glory. Stand with me as I am being prepared to meet our Lord. Mother, your perfection was instantaneous; mine is a process. Be my guide, helping me to cooperate with God's action toward my perfection, so that on the day when God calls me, I will be ready.

Fourth Sorrowful Glorious - Lay the Roses

Mother Mary, I bind these golden yellow roses with a petition for the grace of perfection and humbly lay this bouquet at your feet.

Fifth Glorious Mystery - The Coronation of Mary as Queen of Heaven and Earth

The glory of heaven, what will it be like? What is it like? Vast, infinite, eternal, and I am just one tiny speck in all of creation. Yet, You want me there with You, Lord. You have a special place in mind for me, and You are preparing it for me.

Fifth Glorious Mystery - Lay the Roses

Mother Mary, I bind these golden yellow roses with a petition for the grace of eternal peace and humbly lay this bouquet at your feet.

Day 36

First Joyful Mystery - The Annunciation

I am in prayer waiting on the Lord, open to whatever He has for me. I see His angel before me. He has sent His messenger to me. The angel greets me by name, by God's name for me. I am amazed at first but realize that I am not surprised. There is a familiarity in the greeting, a recognition in the name that brings me joy. The angel proceeds to speak God's message to me.

First Joyful Mystery - Lay the Roses

Mother Mary, I bind these pale blue roses with a petition for the grace of recognizing God's call and humbly lay this bouquet at your feet.

Second Joyful Mystery - The Visitation

Mary, the Mother of God, brings the presence of the Trinity into my home, into my life. She enters softly yet radiantly, with praise and giving glory to God in her gentle, humble, and loving way. She shows me how to welcome and live with all Three Persons of the Trinity. Mary quietly toils in the background, helping me while God goes to work in my heart. She takes care of the other things, so I do not need to worry about them. She keeps me free from distractions so I can welcome God in. I hear Him speak my name in my heart.

Second Joyful Mystery - Lay the Roses

Mother Mary, I bind these pale blue roses with a petition for the grace of your help and humbly lay this bouquet at your feet.

Third Joyful Mystery - The Birth of Jesus

I am on a journey. It is difficult at times, and I do not know how long it will take. I know my final destination, but I do not always know the way. I am not alone though. God is with me through it all. Sometimes He walks with me. Other times He carries me. He gives me others to help along the way. But He always guides me, calling to me by my name. And He allows me to share in the experience of the great mystery of His presence in the world and all the beauty and joy that comes with it.

Third Joyful Mystery - Lay the Roses

Mother Mary, I bind these pale blue roses with a petition for the grace of guidance and humbly lay this bouquet at your feet.

Fourth Joyful Mystery - The Presentation in the Temple

I stand outside the church unsure if I will enter. I know I should, but I am uneasy. I think of all the other things I could be doing. I feel the world trying to pull me back. Then I hear a sound, more within my heart than my ears. I hear my name being called. "I am waiting for you. I Am here for you." The doors of the church open along with the doors of my heart.

Fourth Joyful Mystery - Lay the Roses

Mother Mary, I bind these pale blue roses with a petition for the grace of participation in the life of God and humbly lay this bouquet at your feet.

Fifth Joyful Mystery - The Finding of Jesus in the Temple

I have celebrated with you, Lord. I am happy and content with my life as I continue on my journey home. But as I become caught up into the world again, I realize that I lose sight of You. I want to continue following the crowd even though I feel a tiny tug in another direction. Your presence calls to me, calls out my name. I turn and follow Your voice. I return to You.

Fifth Joyful Mystery - Lay the Roses

Mother Mary, I bind these pale blue roses with a petition for the grace of staying focused on God and humbly lay this bouquet at your feet.

Day 37

First Sorrowful Mystery - The Agony of Jesus in the Garden

I am in the garden. It is dark; I feel dark. I am weighed down with the cares on my heart. Jesus approaches me. He calls me by name. He kneels down and begins to pray for me. He grasps my hand tightly not wanting to let go. Tears stream down my face.

First Sorrowful Mystery - Lay the Roses
Mother Mary, I bind these violet roses with a petition for the grace of time with God and humbly lay this bouquet at your feet.

Second Sorrowful Mystery - Jesus is Scourged at the Pillar

I am at the pillar of scourging. The chains that bind await me. The pillar has my name on it, and I am frightened. I feel a hand on my shoulder. I turn to see Jesus smiling at me. "I am here for you. I take this for you." He says my name. "Do not be afraid."

Second Sorrowful Mystery - Lay the Roses

Mother Mary, I bind these violet roses with a petition for the grace of freedom from fear and humbly lay this bouquet at your feet.

Third Sorrowful Mystery - Jesus is Crowned with Thorns

I stand by myself as others circle about me. They are mocking me and jeering, calling me names. Then I hear my true name called. Jesus is there offering me His hand. He removes the ugly crown from my head and disposes of it. He frees me from the anguish and embraces me as His own.

Third Sorrowful Mystery - Lay the Roses

Mother Mary, I bind these violet roses with a petition for the grace of liberation and humbly lay this bouquet at your feet.

Fourth Sorrowful Mystery - Jesus Carries His Cross

I stand waiting to make my way through the jeering crowd. I feel alone and afraid and weak. The cross I have to carry seems so weighed down. I reach out to pick it up, but a hand stretches past me. Jesus is there to take my cross for me. "It is mine," He says to me. "You are mine." He calls me by my name.

Fourth Sorrowful Mystery - Lay the Roses

Mother Mary, I bind these violet roses with a petition for the grace of giving burdens to God and humbly lay this bouquet at your feet.

Fifth Sorrowful Mystery - The Crucifixion and Death of our Lord Jesus Christ

I await my punishment at the Place of the Skull. The nails lie on the ground. The wood bearing my name anticipates my presence. My sins yell out to me from its rough surface. As I stare at it, my name slowly fades from the cross and Jesus' name appears. "This is My place, not yours." "But they are my sins," I tell Him. "Let Me take them from you."

Fifth Sorrowful Mystery - Lay the Roses
Mother Mary, I bind these violet roses with a petition for the grace of redemption and humbly lay this bouquet at your feet.

Day 38

First Glorious Mystery - The Resurrection of Jesus

I am walking along the road alone, confused and thinking God is gone, that He is dead. Someone approaches me from behind, hurrying to catch up with me. I hear my name and turn to see Him. He inquires about me, genuinely concerned. He accompanies me, looks at me with love, telling me what I need to hear. I listen to Him and learn, my heart burning within me.

Jesus spends as much time with me as I need, helping me to understand. As I watch His face, He reveals His true self to me, unveiling something about my true self as well. I have a great desire to return from where I came and share Him with everyone.

First Glorious Mystery - Lay the Roses

Mother Mary, I bind these pure white roses with a petition for the grace of knowing myself through God and humbly lay this bouquet at your feet.

Second Glorious Mystery - The Ascension of Jesus into Heaven

I stand on the top of the mountain looking out and waiting. Jesus approaches me and calls to me by my name. I turn to face Him. As I look at Him, He sees my concern. He reminds me that He is always with me "in here" and touches my forehead. "I am also here," and He touches my heart. As He looks at me, He communicates the presence of His burning love to me.

Jesus' presence penetrates my heart and soul with His touch. "I am always in here," He says to me again. He looks deep into my soul. "This is where you can go to find me." With His touch, He opens wider the door to my inner room. "I dwell here always. I created this space inside of you for Me."

Second Glorious Mystery - Lay the Roses

Mother Mary, I bind these pure white roses with a petition for the grace of finding God within and humbly lay this bouquet at your feet.

Third Glorious Mystery - The Descent of the Holy Spirit

I am alone in the upper room. I have been praying. I look out the window at the mountain where I last saw Jesus, where He touched me. I experience that burning sensation again. This time it comes not only from inside but also from around me. I feel the air swirl and the rumbling of the walls. I sense the heat as God comes closer to me.

It is a comforting warmth that not only surrounds me but envelopes me. I see the large flame as it descends and comes to rest on me. The love of God is being poured into me once again. He is with me, within me as He promised. I welcome this presence, open myself to Him, listen to Him. I am set afire anew.

Third Glorious Mystery - Lay the Roses

Mother Mary, I bind these pure white roses with a petition for the grace of active faith and humbly lay this bouquet at your feet.

Fourth Glorious Mystery - The Assumption of Mary into Heaven

I do not really know what the end of your life was like, dear Mother. You were free from all sin, perfect in every way. You would not have experienced death in a painful or fearful way. It would have been more like a gentle transition from one state of existence to another. One moment you were here, then as God called, you were fully with

Him, present with Him in all His glory. Stand with me as I am being prepared to meet our Lord. Mother, your perfection was instantaneous; mine is a process. Be my guide, helping me to cooperate with God's action toward my perfection, so that on the day when God calls me, I will be ready.

With my face turned toward you, Lord, my hands and heart are open, my ears are waiting. Speak your words of love to me again. I never tire of hearing them. They help to form me into Your perfect child. They tell me who I am in Your sight. Even in my imperfect nature, I cling to You. I am made whole by You. You make me who I am.

Fourth Glorious Mystery - Lay the Roses

Mother Mary, I bind these pure white roses with a petition for the grace of formation and humbly lay this bouquet at your feet.

Fifth Glorious Mystery - The Coronation of Mary as Queen of Heaven and Earth

The glory of heaven, what will it be like? What is it like? Vast, infinite, eternal, and I am just one tiny speck in all of creation. Yet, You want me there with you, Lord. You have a special place in mind for me, and You are preparing it for me.

Me, the one You have loved with an everlasting love. The one whom You spoke into existence with the name that only You know. The child that You have made Yours. As You long for me, so I long for You. I seek Your face, Lord, that will bring me eternal joy and light.

Fifth Glorious Mystery - Lay the Roses

Mother Mary, I bind these pure white roses with a petition for the grace of eternal joy and humbly lay this bouquet at your feet.

Day 39

First Luminous Mystery - The Baptism of Jesus

I stand staring at the waters. I see myself before I am cleansed. God is waiting for me, the Father who created me wants to recreate me anew. He calls my name, "Come." I am under the water. I release everything to God in that moment of total surrender. Jesus is there to save me. We rise together. He looks me in the eyes. I see His face as He breathes His life into me. I am a new creation, forever changed.

First Luminous Mystery - Lay the Roses

Mother Mary, I bind these orange roses with a petition for the grace of renewal and humbly lay this bouquet at your feet.

Second Luminous Mystery - The Wedding at Cana

I approach the door of the wedding feast to which I have been invited. Jesus is there waiting for me. He smiles and says my name as He welcomes me in. When I enter, it is only the two of us. I am the one being celebrated. Jesus, the Bridegroom, has prepared the abundant feast. He looks at me. "It is all for you."

Second Luminous Mystery - Lay the Roses

Mother Mary, I bind these orange roses with a petition for the grace of union with God and humbly lay this bouquet at your feet.

Third Luminous Mystery - The Proclamation of the Kingdom of God

Jesus is teaching today. I want to hear Him. I follow footprints to the bottom of the mountain. I can hear His voice beckoning me, calling to me by name. I ascend to Him. Jesus is there waiting for me, smiling with His arms open in welcome. I am the only one there. His message is just for me today. "I am here for you." I sit and listen intently to what He has to say.

Third Luminous Mystery - Lay the Roses

Mother Mary, I bind these orange roses with a petition for the grace of understanding and humbly lay this bouquet at your feet.

Fourth Luminous Mystery - The Transfiguration

Once again, I stand at the bottom of the mountain. I look up unsure if I know the way. Can I make it? Then the path opens up for me. Jesus is there to lead and to walk with me. He calls my name and takes my hand. We walk together. At the top, He turns to look at me. As His smile spreads across His face, so does His glory spread across His body. His entire being radiates light. I feel it, the warmth and the love. God's Light envelopes me.

Fourth Luminous Mystery - Lay the Roses

Mother Mary, I bind these orange roses with a petition for the grace of God's light and humbly lay this bouquet at your feet.

Fifth Luminous Mystery - The Institution of the Eucharist

I stand outside the upper room. Once more, Jesus has prepared a special meal for me. "I have longed to celebrate this with you," He says as He calls my name. I accept His invitation again. The table seems sparse this time. "We have all we need," He says to me. I recline at the table with Him. Jesus takes the bread and the wine. I watch His face as He blesses them. "This is for you. I am for you." He looks me in the eyes as He shares Himself with me. His Presence is all I need. Then He lets me rest my head against His chest.

Fifth Luminous Mystery - Lay the Roses

Mother Mary, I bind these orange roses with a petition for the grace of receiving from the Lord and humbly lay this bouquet at your feet.

Day 40

First Sorrowful Mystery - The Agony of Jesus in the Garden

I am in the garden. It is dark; I feel dark. I am weighed down with the cares on my heart. Jesus approaches me. He calls me by name. He kneels down and begins to pray for me. He grasps my hand tightly not wanting to let go. Tears stream down my face.

Jesus and I are in the garden together. As He prays for me, I am praying with Him. He sees my needs and moves closer, puts His arms around me. He turns me to face Him and looks into my eyes. He sees into my heart and soul, speaks to them. I see the love on His face and hear His words in my being.

First Sorrowful Mystery - Lay the Roses

Mother Mary, I bind these blood red roses with a petition for the grace of listening to God and humbly lay this bouquet at your feet.

Second Sorrowful Mystery - Jesus is Scourged at the Pillar

I am at the pillar of scourging. The chains that bind await me. The pillar has my name on it, and I am frightened. I feel a hand on my shoulder. I turn to see Jesus smiling at me. "I am here for you. I take this for you." He says my name. "Do not be afraid."

Jesus takes my place at the pillar. "This is for you. I am for you. I will never abandon you. Let Me be with you always." I see the look of love on His face, in His eyes. He does this willingly and even happily for me. As Jesus endures the pain, I feel my pain slip away. The blows to His body relieve my body. I am His.

Second Sorrowful Mystery - Lay the Roses

Mother Mary, I bind these blood red roses with a petition for the grace of restoration by God and humbly lay this bouquet at your feet.

Third Sorrowful Mystery - Jesus is Crowned with Thorns

I stand by myself as others circle about me. They are mocking me and jeering, calling me names. Then I hear my true name called. Jesus is there offering me His hand. He removes the ugly crown from my head and disposes of it. He frees me from the anguish and embraces me as His own.

Jesus looks at me. I see myself reflected in His eyes. "You are not who they say you are. You are who I say you are. I know the true you. You are mine and always will be." The words of Jesus are seared into my soul.

Third Sorrowful Mystery - Lay the Roses

Mother Mary, I bind these blood red roses with a petition for the grace of receiving identity from God and humbly lay this bouquet at your feet.

Fourth Sorrowful Mystery - Jesus Carries His Cross

I stand waiting to make my way through the jeering crowd. I feel alone and afraid and weak. The cross I have to carry seems so weighed down. I reach out to pick it up, but a hand stretches past me. Jesus is there to take my cross for me. "It is mine," He says to me. "You are mine." He calls me by my name.

I see Jesus' face as He lifts the wood and places it on His shoulder. He motions me ahead. He walks behind me wherever I go, showing the world that He is carrying my burdens, that He is with me always. The crowd steps back giving us room. I hold up my head.

Fourth Sorrowful Mystery - Lay the Roses

Mother Mary, I bind these blood red roses with a petition for the grace of confidence in God's help and humbly lay this bouquet at your feet.

Fifth Sorrowful Mystery - The Crucifixion and Death of our Lord Jesus Christ

I await my punishment at the Place of the Skull. The nails lie on the ground. The wood bearing my name anticipates my presence. My sins yell out to me from its rough surface. As I stare at it, my name slowly fades from the cross and Jesus' name appears. "This is my place, not yours." "But they are My sins," I tell Him. "Let Me take them from you."

I see Jesus lovingly place Himself onto my cross. "It is all for love of you. I take away your sins. I have won you. You are mine. You belong completely to Me now. The enemy who knows your name but calls you by your sin has lost. God knows you and loves you. I call you by your true name." And I hear His name for me again from His lips.

Fifth Sorrowful Mystery - Lay the Roses

Mother Mary, I bind these blood red roses with a petition for the grace of belonging to God and humbly lay this bouquet at your feet.

Day 41

First Joyful Mystery - The Annunciation

I am in prayer waiting on the Lord, open to whatever He has for me. I see His angel before me. He has sent His messenger to me. The angel greets me by name, by God's name for me. I am amazed at first but realize that I am not surprised. There is a familiarity in the greeting, a recognition in the name that brings me joy. The angel proceeds to speak God's message to me.

I kneel before the angel of God who has come to deliver His message to me. My heart is open to God my Father. I say yes to Him. "Fiat," let it be done; Your will, O Lord. His Spirit fills me. Jesus is alive in me. The Most Holy Trinity makes its home in me, in my heart.

First Joyful Mystery - Lay the Roses

Mother Mary, I bind these pale pink roses with a petition for the grace of receptivity and humbly lay this bouquet at your feet.

Second Joyful Mystery - The Visitation

Mary, the Mother of God, brings the presence of the Trinity into my home, into my life. She enters softly yet radiantly, with praise and giving glory to God in her gentle, humble, and loving way. She shows me how to welcome and live with all Three Persons of the Trinity. Mary quietly toils in the background, helping me while God goes to work in my heart. She takes care of the other things, so I do not need to worry about them. She keeps me free from distractions so I can welcome God in. I hear Him speak my name in my heart.

God knows what my needs are, what I should hear from Him. So, I am quiet and let Him speak. He is patient with me as His life grows within me. He takes as long as it requires. Growth can be a slow process. He opens my ears so I can hear. When the time is right, He opens my mouth so I can praise

Him. His work in my soul fills me with joy. His presence makes me want to dance and sing of His might and glory.

Second Joyful Mystery - Lay the Roses

Mother Mary, I bind these pale pink roses with a petition for the grace of listening and humbly lay this bouquet at your feet.

Third Joyful Mystery - The Birth of Jesus

I am on a journey. It is difficult at times, and I do not know how long it will take. I know my final destination, but I do not always know the way. I am not alone though. God is with me through it all. Sometimes He walks with me. Other times He carries me. He gives me others to help along the way. But He always guides me, calling to me by my name. And He allows me to share in the experience of the great mystery of His presence in the world and all the beauty and joy that comes with it.

God gives beautiful moments along the journey to show His love for me. I find myself outside the stable in Bethlehem. A soft warm glow emanates from within. I enter quietly. All is still. Mary and Joseph are asleep. Even the animals are resting. I walk up to the manger and look inside. I see the newborn Jesus swaddled and snug in the hay. I stare in awe at His sweet small face as He sleeps. He slowly stretches and opens His eyes. A tiny smile seems to form on His lips. A little hand appears from the cloth moving upward as if He is reaching toward me. I gently lift Him from his temporary bed and hold him against my chest. He places His head against my heart and falls back to sleep.

Third Joyful Mystery - Lay the Roses

Mother Mary, I bind these pale pink roses with a petition for the grace of the peace of resting with God and humbly lay this bouquet at your feet.

Fourth Joyful Mystery - The Presentation in the Temple

I stand outside the church unsure if I will enter. I know I should, but I am uneasy. I think of all the other things I could be doing. I feel the world trying to pull me back. Then I hear a sound, more within my heart than my ears. I hear my name being called. "I am waiting for you. I Am here for you." The doors of the church open along with the doors of my heart.

I enter the church to find my Lord Jesus on the altar. Light is streaming from Him. "I am here night and day waiting for you to come to Me." I stay with Him, kneeling in worship, letting Him guide my prayer, listening to His words to me.

Fourth Joyful Mystery - Lay the Roses

Mother Mary, I bind these pale pink roses with a petition for the grace of adoration and humbly lay this bouquet at your feet.

Fifth Joyful Mystery - The Finding in the Temple

I have celebrated with you, Lord. I am happy and content with my life as I continue on my journey home. But as I become caught up into the world again, I realize that I lose sight of You. I want to continue following the crowd even though I feel a tiny tug in another direction. Your presence calls to me, calls out my name. I turn and follow Your voice. I return to You.

I am seeking You in a world that has lost You. I return to the temple of my heart. It is there that You always dwell. "Did you not know that is where I would be?" I sit down in the place You have reserved for me, and I listen to You.

Fifth Joyful Mystery - Lay the Roses

Mother Mary, I bind these pale pink roses with a petition for the grace of finding God and humbly lay this bouquet at your feet.

Week 7

I hope that last week you were able to make some connections with God and encounter Him in your inner room. Hopefully you heard Him speak your name and were able to contemplate the face of Jesus. Now that we are more open to Him, God wants to help us to experience His healing. We all need some type of healing. It is difficult to let ourselves be vulnerable, but God already knows where we need Him. Let's just allow Him to do what He desires to do in us. Try to fully enter into the experience that Jesus wants to have with you in the meditations.

Welcome the love and the healing that He offers.

Day 42

First Glorious Mystery - The Resurrection of Jesus

I stand outside the tomb weeping. I have been looking for Jesus, but I can't find Him. I need Him. I hear something behind me and turn around. Someone is there, but I do not know who it is. Then He calls my name, and I recognize Him. I truly see Him for who He is. And I know that He sees me for who I am and for who I am able to be.

He looks at me and asks me if I love Him. I tell Him that I do. Jesus tells me not to hold on to my old ways of living but to let Him show me who I can be, made whole by Him. He holds up His hands with the light shining forth from them. He places His hands on me and I feel His resurrected Spirit flow into me, offering me healing and a new beginning.

First Glorious Mystery - Lay the Roses

Mother Mary, I bind these golden yellow roses with a petition for the grace of new life and humbly lay this bouquet at your feet.

Second Glorious Mystery - The Ascension of Jesus into Heaven

I am waiting with Jesus before He ascends. "My peace I give to you. You can have it always." Jesus breathes on me. He places His hands on me in a blessing that goes to the core of my being. The blessing continues when He begins to ascend. As He rises, my heart rises with Him. Glory and light stream from heaven upon me.

Second Glorious Mystery - Lay the Roses

Mother Mary, I bind these golden yellow roses with a petition for the grace of blessing and humbly lay this bouquet at your feet.

Third Glorious Mystery - The Descent of the Holy Spirit

The Holy Spirit descends upon me. The burning and purifying presence of God intensifies in me. The same Spirit that raised Jesus from the dead lives in me, raising me to new life with Him. His presence is a cleansing fire that purifies me, burning away from me what is not holy and pure. The flame is God's hand upon me and within me, purging and healing, reviving and strengthening.

Third Glorious Mystery - Lay the Roses

Mother Mary, I bind these golden yellow roses with a petition for the grace of cleansing and humbly lay this bouquet at your feet.

Fourth Glorious Mystery - The Assumption of Mary into Heaven

I bask in the light from Mary's path to heaven. I stand before You, Lord, as You speak Your words of healing to me. I, Your child, am in need of them. My purification is in Your hands. I let it penetrate through my heart, my mind, my body, my soul. I accept Your healing and Your grace.

Fourth Glorious Mystery - Lay the Roses

Mother Mary, I bind these golden yellow roses with a petition for the grace of purification and humbly lay this bouquet at your feet.

Fifth Glorious Mystery - The Coronation of Mary as Queen of Heaven and Earth

Lord, on that day when You call me home, You will shower me with Your light and peace, with Your care and love. Every tear of mine will be wiped away, every sorrow will be turned to joy. All things will be made new. But I also know that You want that for me now, in whatever way I am able to receive. I receive what You offer me, the crown that is mine.

Fifth Glorious Mystery - Lay the Roses

Mother Mary, I bind these golden yellow roses with a petition for the grace of newness of life and humbly lay this bouquet at your feet.

Day 43

First Joyful Mystery - The Annunciation

I have said yes to God, given Him my Fiat. The Trinity, God Most Holy lives in me. "We want to make you whole, one, like Us." God's presence fills my entire being, purging what should not be there, removing all that is not of God, filling me with grace. God is healing, cleansing, and restoring. I allow God to work and love and grow in me.

First Joyful Mystery - Lay the Roses

Mother Mary, I bind these pale blue roses with a grace for the virtue of restoration and humbly lay this bouquet at your feet.

Second Joyful Mystery - The Visitation

The Lord continues working in my inner room. There are more things that need to be done. A dwelling for God should be immaculate, so I invite Mary in to help Him. As He cleanses the interior, the doubt and fear fall away. Any disgrace is left behind. He replenishes what is lacking. He calms the anxieties. Any pain and desolation I feel, He faces with me. He heals my interior wounds.

Second Joyful Mystery - Lay the Roses

Mother Mary, I bind these pale blue roses with a petition for the grace of healing and humbly lay this bouquet at your feet.

Third Joyful Mystery - The Birth of Jesus

Baby Jesus is sleeping against my chest. I feel His tiny breaths as He exhales. I instinctively inhale to receive. Each breath of His becomes mine, from His body into mine. This life-giving breath sends His Spirit deep into my being, rejuvenating me from the inside out. His tiny Heart so close to mine beats in unison with my heart that is in need of His healing. His new life is giving me new life.

Third Joyful Mystery - Lay the Roses

Mother Mary, I bind these pale blue roses with a petition for the grace of renewal and humbly lay this bouquet at your feet.

Fourth Joyful Mystery - The Presentation in the Temple

Jesus is always there for me in the church. He is always here for me in the temple of my heart. He is my light and my glory. He pierces my heart to purify it, to cleanse it, and to heal it. Then He refills it with His love.

Fourth Joyful Mystery - Lay the Roses

Mother Mary, I bind these pale blue roses with a petition for the grace of purification and humbly lay this bouquet at your feet.

Fifth Joyful Mystery - The Finding in the Temple

I have found you, Jesus, in Your Father's house. This is the house that He created for You, my heart, my inner room. In this house of Yours, Jesus, this home of ours, I give You free reign to do what needs to be done. I pledge obedience to You. I accept Your words, Your gifts, and Your healing. I keep it all in my heart.

Fifth Joyful Mystery - Lay the Roses

Mother Mary, I bind these pale blue roses with a petition for the grace of life with Jesus and humbly lay this bouquet at your feet.

Day 44

First Sorrowful Mystery - The Agony of Jesus in the Garden

As I kneel in the garden praying, I am taken back to the first garden where everything was perfect, before sin entered the world. The Lord stands before me wanting to make me whole again. As He places His hands on my head, I feel my anxieties flow from me to Him. He absorbs my agony and makes it His own. When I feel empty, He refills me, flooding me with His healing presence.

First Sorrowful Mystery - Lay the Roses

Mother Mary, I bind these violet roses with a petition for the grace of calmness and humbly lay this bouquet at your feet.

Second Sorrowful Mystery - Jesus is Scourged at the Pillar

Jesus takes on the scourging of His flesh to make reparation for my sins, especially those of the flesh. With every lash He receives, I feel more strength to resist temptation. Every wound of His begins the healing of one of my wounds. The more He suffers, the more I am healed, until I gleam with purity. It is possible for me. Jesus makes it possible.

Second Sorrowful Mystery - Lay the Roses

Mother Mary, I bind these violet roses with a petition for the grace of purity and humbly lay this bouquet at your feet.

Third Sorrowful Mystery - Jesus is Crowned with Thorns

After removing my crown of disgrace, Jesus places His hands on my head, curing the lacerations from the thorns. I feel His power penetrate, healing the wounds of my mind and the lies that I have believed. The insults and anguish that I have allowed to control my life are gone. Jesus is King of my life, and I now live for Him.

Third Sorrowful Mystery - Lay the Roses

Mother Mary, I bind these violet roses with a petition for the grace of living as a child of the King and humbly lay this bouquet at your feet.

Fourth Sorrowful Mystery - Jesus Carries His Cross

The cross I have carried in my life has left me with many injuries. Some are sores that are still open. Some are old and scabbed over. A few, though only scars on the surface, continue to fester inside. Jesus wants to get to the heart of all my pain to cure the infection, remove the splinters, clear the scars, and create a beautiful new surface.

Fourth Sorrowful Glorious - Lay the Roses

Mother Mary, I bind these violet roses with a petition for the grace of healing and humbly lay this bouquet at your feet.

Fifth Sorrowful Mystery - The Crucifixion and Death of our Lord Jesus Christ

I stand with Jesus near the empty cross. I stretch out my arms toward Him, not the wood. My hands which should have received the nails now only receive His embrace. My feet that should have been fixed to the cross, journey with His feet. My heart that should have been pierced with a lance is opened by His love. The complete emptying that Jesus experiences on the cross, the pouring out of all His Blood, is to fill me with His life. Blood equals life, and He gives His for me. He leaves nothing for Himself. His total self-sacrifice is so I can live.

Fifth Sorrowful Mystery - Lay the Roses

Mother Mary, I bind these violet roses with a petition for the grace of life and humbly lay this bouquet at your feet.

Day 45

First Glorious Mystery - The Resurrection of Jesus

Risen Jesus, I see You stand before me. Your arms are open in love and welcome. You look different, yet You help me to recognize that it is You, Jesus, who have touched me in so many ways. Can it really be? Then You speak to me, "Let me show you. These are the feet which travel with you throughout your journey. Since the path isn't easy at times, My feet have been pierced to relieve your steps. See My hands, the ones which reach out to you. The nails have kept us united and steady. Here is My side, split open for My mercy to flow upon you. It remains open so that you always have access to My Heart. Look inside. See My Heart beating for love of you. Let it beat for yours when it feels unable to beat on its own.

First Glorious Mystery - Lay the Roses

Mother Mary, I bind these pure white roses with a petition for the grace of unity with Christ and humbly lay this bouquet at your feet.

Second Glorious Mystery - The Ascension of Jesus into Heaven

Jesus, You take me by the hand and we walk together, side by side. You are right next to me, always with me. "I will remain here always, even if you can't see me."

Our walk takes us higher until we stand above all else. The clouds surround us, yet I can see clearly both the earth and heaven. The Kingdom is open to me, even as I stand here on the ground. "You always have access to the Heavenly Realm. I brought that to you. And I do not take it away. It is always here with you."

You show me Your wounds once again, aglow with light. "I do not hide my wounds, nor do I remove them. They are a part of Me now. They have made me who I am and who you are. I received them to give you life and to heal your wounds. They have no power over either of us. They contain power and life for you. Here, unite your wounds with Mine." The light from within Jesus, that is also from heaven and a part of the earth, flows within me too, as we all become one.

Second Glorious Mystery - Lay the Roses

Mother Mary, I bind these pure white roses with a petition for the grace of unity with heaven and humbly lay this bouquet at your feet.

Third Glorious Mystery - The Descent of the Holy Spirit

The lights slowly fade from around me and the clouds disperse. I no longer see Jesus with my eyes, yet I know that He is still here. I feel Him in my Heart. I pray in thanksgiving and praise. As my prayer comes from within me, I feel my heart open in joy. My prayer of praise and thanksgiving begins simply yet is pure and true, for God has been so good to me. I feel Mary join me and we sing our song of love together.

As the air begins to swirl around me, my song, my prayer intensifies. The joy inside joins with the song of praise from heaven. It is the Holy Spirit that unites me and my prayer to heaven. I feel the Lord speak. "My presence is what makes you whole, who you are. It gives you your identity. Let My love inflame your heart as I remove from you any fear, doubt, hesitation, anxiety. I place in you My Spirit, which fills you with peace, confidence, knowledge, and so much more. All you need comes from Me."

Third Glorious Mystery - Lay the Roses

Mother Mary, I bind these pure white roses with a petition for the grace of indwelling of God and humbly lay this bouquet at your feet.

Fourth Glorious Mystery - The Assumption of Mary into Heaven

The united song from my heart and heaven slowly begins to soften until there is just a gentle prayer on my lips. The wind has calmed and brought with it a peaceful covering of clouds once again. There is still one other voice praying with me. I hear the sweet gentle words of Mother Mary. I do not see her, yet she speaks to me in her prayer. "I am here, dear child. Like our Lord, I too am always with you. As your Mother, I can never be away from you. I spread my arms, and my mantle shelters you. My veil hangs between heaven and earth. You may not always know what happens on the other side, but at times it is lifted for you. I always hold you in my arms here on earth, but I look forward to the day when you come running to greet me in heaven.

Fourth Glorious Mystery - Lay the Roses

Mother Mary, I bind these pure white roses with a petition for the grace of hope in heaven and humbly lay this bouquet at your feet.

Fifth Glorious Mystery - The Coronation of Mary as Queen of Heaven and Earth

Mother Mary continues her lovely song, "Yes, my veil hangs down from heaven, but you are able to see through it and even reach through when God allows. Heaven is always open to you. I too am on both sides. I am where you need me to be. I will be either standing with you in prayer, service, and love or I am interceding for you to My Son. Your Queen never forgets you and neither does your King. You are a part of that Kingdom now. What awaits you in heaven is the full realization of your citizenship. But I share my throne with you whenever you need a reminder of who you are and Whose you are. Live in our Love.

Fifth Glorious Mystery - Lay the Roses

Mother Mary, I bind these pure white roses with a petition for the grace of glory of heaven and humbly lay this bouquet at your feet.

Day 46

First Luminous Mystery - The Baptism of Jesus

I stand beside the river. I see Jesus in the water. He has received His baptism. He has sanctified the water for me. Jesus is aglow with the presence of the Holy Spirit. He reaches out His hand to me and speaks. "Come, My child. Do not be afraid. I, your Jesus, am here for you. Come to Me. Enter the cleansing and healing waters with Me." I step forward toward Jesus. He cups His hands and fills them with the sparkling water. I close my eyes and He lets it flow onto my head and over my entire body. I feel a lightness as I am being washed anew. As the flow continues, I open my eyes to see that the drops of water are now Jesus' tears of joy at my rebirth with Him.

First Luminous Mystery - Lay the Roses

Mother Mary, I bind these orange roses with a petition for the grace of cleansing and humbly lay this bouquet at your feet.

Second Luminous Mystery - The Wedding at Cana

I am sitting at the head table at the banquet of the wedding feast. All those around me are celebrating, enjoying themselves. There is much activity. Yet, I do not feel a part of it. I feel separated and distant, as if I am encompassed in my own bubble of stillness. I look down at my place at the table and it is empty. I have nothing with which to celebrate. But I am not sure what it is that I lack. I look to the back of the room and see Mary, also a part of this air of quietude. She sees me, is watching me. As she smiles softly, I feel her exude peace. Mary turns her head toward her Son and my eyes follow. She smiles in a most beautiful and knowing way. All else fades away as Jesus approaches me. He says to me, "I have what you need, My beloved." He holds out His hands to me. They are open in offering. I reach out to Him.

Second Luminous Mystery - Lay the Roses

Mother Mary, I bind these orange roses with a petition for the grace of receiving from the Lord and humbly lay this bouquet at your feet.

Third Luminous Mystery - The Proclamation of the Kingdom of God

I am walking alone in a desert, and I am not sure where I am going. It seems barren and parched. I am heading someplace, but I do not know where or even how to get there. The dusty air swirls around me and I feel dry. I sit down on a rock, unsure of what to do next. Then I sense a gentle hand on my shoulder. I turn and look into the face of Jesus. He smiles at me. His eyes are aglow with love. Jesus says to me, "I am here for you. This is why I have come." He takes my chin in His hand and looks intently at me, seeing inside of me and knowing my needs. He places His other hand on my head and begins to pray.

Third Luminous Mystery - Lay the Roses

Mother Mary, I bind these orange roses with a petition for the grace of recovery and humbly lay this bouquet at your feet.

Fourth Luminous Mystery - The Transfiguration

I stand on the mountain top, eyes closed, face upturned, arms outstretched. I feel different, vulnerable, yet safe because I feel You here, Jesus. As the wind blows around me, I begin to breathe more deeply. With every inhale, You give new life to me. Every exhale, I release to You what I do not need. Jesus, Your peace fills not only my lungs but my very soul. I hear the song of heaven singing over me.

Then I feel Your warmth, Jesus, as it floats over and around me. I take comfort in Your presence. I hear you say to me, "Look at Me. See

Me as I truly am." I open my eyes to Your glory, Jesus. You are reality, what truly matters. I receive Your light and allow it to guide me.

Fourth Luminous Mystery - Lay the Roses

Mother Mary, I bind these orange roses with a petition for the grace of the light of Christ and humbly lay this bouquet at your feet.

Fifth Luminous Mystery - The Institution of the Eucharist

Jesus, You take me by the hand and lead me back to the wedding banquet, to the table set for us. You seat me on a cushion next to You. This time the table is not empty, though the meal is simple, bread and wine. I hear You bless the meal. Then You offer it to me.

You say to me, "I have sacrificed Myself for you, all that I have and all that I am. I have given Myself for you." Then, Jesus, You stoop down to take my feet in Your precious Hands. You lovingly wash them and dry them with a cloth. "There is nothing I wouldn't do for you. I have seen where you have been and I wish to journey with you now." You lead me to the door. As we step out together, Jesus, You remind me, "We are in Communion, so I remain with you always!"

Fifth Luminous Mystery - Lay the Roses

Mother Mary, I bind these orange roses with a petition for the grace of communion with God and humbly lay this bouquet at your feet.

Day 47

First Sorrowful Mystery - The Agony of Jesus in the Garden

I sit and weep as I wait in the garden. My sorrows seem deep at times. I feel I am alone, as if no one cares. Yet when I look up, You are there, Jesus. You kneel down beside me and put a hand on mine. With Your other hand You wipe away a tear. Then I notice a tear on Your face. "I am here for you. I understand. I care. Let Me heal your sorrows."

My tears fall into Your open hand, where they shimmer. I see You peer into the tiny pool of water. You take Your finger and swirl it around, adding Your healing touch to my memories, my concerns, my hurts. Then I watch You blow on them. Slowly the water begins to evaporate into tiny droplets that ascend to the Father.

First Sorrowful Mystery - Lay the Roses

Mother Mary, I bind these blood red roses with a petition for the grace of giving my worries to God and humbly lay this bouquet at your feet.

Second Sorrowful Mystery - Jesus is Scourged at the Pillar

Jesus, You stand before me after Your scourging. I see how Your body is torn open and bleeding. I feel so sad because I know You suffered this torture for me. You are in great pain. You understand when I am too. As I approach, You look at me with love but also with pleading. Your eyes move toward a clean white cloth and bowl of fresh water on the ground next to You, and You nod to me weakly. I take the cloth, kiss it, and dip it into the bowl, soaking up the water. Then I gently begin to wipe the blood and dirt from Your mangled body. I see You wince in pain at first, yet You urge me to keep going. I periodically rinse the bloodied and soiled cloth in the bowl, yet the water always remains clear and fresh. The bowl stays full. As I continue working and the water runs over Your precious body, the open wounds slowly begin to close and fade. I also notice in the process of helping You, Jesus, that my wounds are starting to feel better. We are both becoming stronger and healthier, more whole.

By the time I finish, Your skin is perfect and completely whole once again. The transformation that took place on my Lord has begun in me. Jesus, You take the cloth, now dry and pristine, kiss it and carefully fold it and place it in my hand for me to keep. Then You welcome me into Your arms.

Second Sorrowful Mystery - Lay the Roses

Mother Mary, I bind these blood red roses with a petition for the grace of physical healing and humbly lay this bouquet at your feet.

Third Sorrowful Mystery - Jesus is Crowned with Thorns

I am sitting alone in the dark. I am bowed down, unable to sit up straight. I feel so weighed down by life sometimes. My head is heavy.

I sense the world spinning around me though I can't see it. It's always there with its noise, distractions, and fast pace. I feel it luring me into its blackness. I do not want to go, but the pull is too strong for me. I barely whisper, "I need help."

Then someone is standing in front of me, blocking it with His presence. Jesus, I see You all aglow in white. You overcome that which tries to drag me in. The dark, which had been draining me, is cut off.

Your light, Jesus, comes close to me and begins to fill me. It completely opposes the blackness. The radiance from Your crown shines on my head, raising it up. I am able to sit up and receive. I hear Your thoughts in my mind: "Beloved child, worthy, wanted, known, beautiful!" I welcome Your soothing hands on my head. They give me relief and comfort. You allow me to rest this way as long as I need.

Third Sorrowful Mystery - Lay the Roses

Mother Mary, I bind these blood red roses with a petition for the grace of emotional healing and humbly lay this bouquet at your feet.

Fourth Sorrowful Mystery - Jesus Carries His Cross

I open the door to begin a new day. Before I can step out, my path is blocked by a large wooden cross. Unsure of what to do, I ask for Your help, Jesus. I hear a sound as if wood is being sawed. Suddenly, a crack appears in the top of the cross, and it splits down the middle and falls apart.

I see You there, Jesus. You reach out and take my hand, leading me onward into the day. In Your hand, which is holding mine, is a very small cross. You wrap my fingers around it and send me forth.

I continue on my way. After a while, I approach another large rough cross blocking my path. This time Jesus, You are on the other side. I watch as You reach around and pull me past the cross to You. I see that You have a medium-sized cross in Your arms. You offer it to me. It is smooth and does not hurt me. I continue on.

Eventually, I see a third large cross along my route. This time Jesus, You are beside me. I almost laugh as You take Your foot and push down the cross. You and I step over it together. Jesus, I notice You carrying a large cross on Your back. You offer it to me. I nod and You gently place one side of the crossbeam on my shoulder. Despite its size, it does not feel heavy. Then You put the other side of the beam on Your shoulder, and we walk on together. Jesus, You and I carry this cross throughout the day.

Fourth Sorrowful Mystery - Lay the Roses

Mother Mary, I bind these blood red roses with a petition for the grace of strength from God and humbly lay this bouquet at your feet.

Fifth Sorrowful Mystery - The Crucifixion and Death of our Lord Jesus Christ

I stand at the edge of a precipice. I cannot recognize what is around me. A dense fog surrounds. I cannot see what is below. All I see is You, Jesus, hanging on the cross at a distance in front of me. A vast, dark openness awaits between us. I feel compelled onward, yet I am afraid. The narrow path behind me is uncertain.

I sense in my heart, "Trust me." I begin to step forward yet hesitate. Then I remember the times that You have been with me, Jesus, drying my tears, hearing my prayers, carrying my cross with me. I open my arms and jump forward. Immediately, my arms are caught by angels, and I am floating on a cloud. The angels carry me to Your open arms, Jesus, which have come off the cross to embrace me. "I am always holding you. Be not afraid."

Fifth Sorrowful Mystery - Lay the Roses

Mother Mary, I bind these blood red roses with a petition for the grace of surrender to God and humbly lay this bouquet at your feet.

Day 48

First Joyful Mystery - The Annunciation

I, your Father, have created you. I can recreate you anew. I placed you in your mother's womb. I knew every aspect of your being, because I determined it all, even before you were. You have always been in My mind, and you always will be. Give, in love, all to Me as I love you. I willed you into being and I keep you in existence. I placed life, My life, inside you. Know that God is living and working in you from within. Allow My healing to come to you from your very depths.

Jesus chose to enter into this life with you. He became vulnerable too, for you. I placed Him here through My Spirit. He dwelt in the protective womb of the Blessed Virgin Mary. She nourished Him with her own body. She wishes to care for you as well, for you are her child too. Let her presence in your life be a womb to surround and comfort you. Allow Mary to protect. Jesus shares her with you.

Love is both within and all around you.

First Joyful Mystery - Lay the Roses

Mother Mary, I bind these pale pink roses with a petition for the grace of protection and humbly lay this bouquet at your feet.

Second Joyful Mystery - The Visitation

As Mary carries you with her, I, Your Father, continue to watch over your care. Since she is ever docile to Me, I guide her actions, which in turn benefit you. You remain encased in our Love, which supports you and leads you.

Through the Holy Spirit, Mary takes you with her, and together you can work for love in the world. I allow your own actions to benefit you too when you reach out in love to those around you. You can give them what they need. But I permit those acts of charity to grant healing to you as well. You can feel this happen. My power is present in you, and you share it with those to whom you are sent. This makes Me more alive in the world but also within you.

Second Joyful Mystery - Lay the Roses

Mother Mary, I bind these pale pink roses with a petition for the grace of a mutual exchange of love and humbly lay this bouquet at your feet.

Third Joyful Mystery - The Birth of Jesus

Mothers are life giving. I allow them to cooperate with Me, the Father, in bringing about new creations. Your Mother Mary is the epitome of this. She is ever open to how I am moving and acting in the world. She brings God to you and to the world in a powerful way. When you remain with her, she shares this with you.

I also create healing in you when you cooperate with Mary's life-giving actions of sharing My Son to others. Giving this gift of Jesus to those who are in need is the most uplifting work. It is the mission of all in My family. There are many in the world who do not know God. Most are seeking, but in the wrong places. Let them find Jesus in the manger of your heart. Then the glory of God will be given not only to them but to you too.

Third Joyful Mystery - Lay the Roses

Mother Mary, I bind these pale pink roses with a petition for the grace of sharing God's love and humbly lay this bouquet at your feet.

Fourth Joyful Mystery - The Presentation in the Temple

As a good Mother, Mary is faithful to God and offers you to Me, the Father. Your whole life can be given to Me through your obedience and faithfulness, just like Mary and Joseph. As with Jesus in the Temple, I give you back to them and their care so they can continue to provide for you as your heavenly and spiritual family.

Then you too can be a light to the world. Your light that shines before others is the presence of Christ within you. Keep that light kindled in prayer and worship of God. Then, the sharing of yourself will give you wholeness and fulfillment.

Fourth Joyful Mystery - Lay the Roses

Mother Mary, I bind these pale pink roses with a petition for the grace of faithfulness and humbly lay this bouquet at your feet.

Fifth Joyful Mystery - The Finding in the Temple

The members of your heavenly family are always available to guide your worship and celebration, for they participate in it with you. Let them accompany you throughout all of life, but especially allow them to guide your spiritual growth. Then you will be able to know and understand the Truth that is God and to live it. When you seem lost, they will find you and bring you back to Me, so I can renew you and give you what you need.

Remember, you can always find Me in the temple of your heart. I am so close to you that I am a part of you. It is easiest to find Me when you let go of all else. Release it all to Me. Sit in the quiet. That is how I speak, in the quiet of your heart. And that is where you find fulfillment.

Fifth Joyful Mystery - Lay the Roses

Mother Mary, I bind these pale pink roses with a petition for the grace of returning to God and humbly lay this bouquet at your feet.

Week 8

Last week's meditations on healing may have brought up some difficult things. Some pain can be very deep. Remember that healing is a process that may take time. There may be areas of profound hurt that will need to be covered in lots of prayer and possibly have the help of a priest or other professional. God desires our wholeness and restoration. He is with us making it happen. Let's be patient with ourselves and let God work in His time.

In this last week of our prayers, we are going to focus on praise and thanksgiving to God for all He is doing through this novena and for allowing us to be a part of it. For the first day, I am going to let God lead you more directly Himself without going through me so we can each praise and thank Him in our own way. I have not written specific meditations for each mystery for day 49 but have included some scripture verses. Let the Holy Spirit prompt you. Praise and thanksgiving go hand in hand. Each of us has our own personal things to thank God for. In the laying of the roses, I left the grace blank for the first day, so you can fill in your own.

For most of the week, my meditations are shorter to allow you more freedom to follow where the Holy Spirit is taking you.

While we are praising and thanking God this week, we will also be looking at how we can go forth from the rosary novena taking with us what God has revealed to us and living our lives according to His most holy will. The novena ends on Friday. The first year we prayed the novena, the last day was the memorial of Saints Martha, Mary, and Lazarus. These three dear friends of Jesus can help us in living our Christian lives. They were very different, yet all shared a close personal relationship with Jesus and with one another. I think we can incorporate the best attributes of these three saints to inspire us in our daily living. So, I have kept them on the meditations for day 54. The three of them were dramatically changed by the presence of Jesus in their lives.

As we finish this rosary novena, let us ask if we have let ourselves be changed by Jesus. Have we invited Jesus into our homes and family lives and into our hearts? Have we developed an intimate relationship with Him to allow transformation to take place? What can we continue to do to keep working on our relationship and further foster our conversion and renewal?

Let us pray...

Day 49

First Glorious Mystery - The Resurrection of Jesus

Jesus told her, "I am the resurrection and the life; whoever believes in me, even if he dies, will live, and everyone who lives and believes in me will never die. Do you believe this?" ~John 11:25-26

I will give thanks to you, Lord, with all my heart; I will tell of all your wonderful deeds. ~Psalm 9:1

First Glorious Mystery - Lay the Roses

Mother Mary, I bind these golden yellow roses with a petition for the grace of _____ and humbly lay this bouquet at your feet.

Second Glorious Mystery – The Ascension of Jesus into Heaven

Jesus Christ has gone into heaven and is at the right hand of God, with angels, authorities, and powers subject to him. ~1 Peter 3:22

Great is the LORD and worthy of much praise, whose grandeur is beyond understanding. ~Psalm 145:3

Second Glorious Mystery - Lay the Roses

Mother Mary, I bind these golden yellow roses with a petition for the grace of _____ and humbly lay this bouquet at your feet.

Third Glorious Mystery - The Descent of the Holy Spirit

This is how we know that we remain in him and he in us, that he has given us of his Spirit. ~1 John 4:13

Praise the Lord, my soul; all my inmost being praise his holy name. ~Psalm 103:1

Third Glorious Mystery - Lay the Roses

Mother Mary, I bind these golden yellow roses with a petition for the grace of _____ and humbly lay this bouquet at your feet.

Fourth Glorious Mystery - The Assumption of Mary into Heaven

Arise, O Lord, into your resting place: you and the ark, which you have sanctified. ~Psalm 132:8

I will extol the Lord at all times; his praise will always be on my lips. ~Psalm 34:1

Fourth Glorious Mystery - Lay the Roses

Mother Mary, I bind these golden yellow roses with a petition for the grace of _____ and humbly lay this bouquet at your feet.

Fifth Glorious Mystery - The Coronation of Mary as Queen of Heaven and Earth

A great sign appeared in the sky, a woman clothed with the sun, with the moon under her feet, and on her head a crown of twelve stars. ~Revelation 12:1

"To him who sits on the throne and to the Lamb be praise and honor and glory and power, for ever and ever!" ~Revelation 5:13

Fifth Glorious Mystery - Lay the Roses

Mother Mary, I bind these golden yellow roses with a petition for the grace of _____ and humbly lay this bouquet at your feet.

Day 50

First Joyful Mystery - The Annunciation

God, You are so good. I praise You for Your goodness. I thank You for the gift of life and for Mary's yes that brought Life into the world. I cooperate with Your plan for my life which connects me to the lives of all others.

Lord, you are my God; I will exalt you and praise your name, for in perfect faithfulness you have done wonderful things, things planned long ago.
~Isaiah 25:1

First Joyful Mystery - Lay the Roses

Mother Mary, I bind these pale blue roses with a petition for the grace of acceptance of God's plan and humbly lay this bouquet at your feet.

Second Joyful Mystery - The Visitation

I praise You and thank You, Lord, for this amazing world and all the wonderful people You have placed in it with me. I am grateful for Mother Mary's example of charity. I will accept hers toward me and share it with others. I will give You glory in all that I do. May it all be for You.

My mouth is filled with your praise, declaring your splendor all day long.~Psalm 71:8

Second Joyful Mystery - Lay the Roses

Mother Mary, I bind these pale blue roses with a petition for the grace of charity and humbly lay this bouquet at your feet.

Third Joyful Mystery - The Birth of Jesus

Father, I am in awe of everything You do, including the humility of Jesus' birth. You show me a simpler way to live through the Holy Family. I choose to be humble and grateful for all I have, focusing on that and not what I think I am lacking. You provide all to me. Thank you!

I will put enmity between you and the woman, and between your offspring and hers; They will strike at your head, while you strike at their heel. ~Genesis 3:15

Third Joyful Mystery - Lay the Roses

Mother Mary, I bind these pale blue roses with a petition for the grace of humble simplicity and humbly lay this bouquet at your feet.

Fourth Joyful Mystery - The Presentation in the Temple

Lord God, I praise You, for it is right and is what I owe to You. But it is also what I desire. I thank You for making Yourself known to the world and to me. I know You are with me always.

I will give thanks to you, Lord, with all my heart; I will tell of all your wonderful deeds. ~Psalm 9:1

Fourth Joyful Mystery - Lay the Roses

Mother Mary, I bind these pale blue roses with a petition for the grace of closeness with God and humbly lay this bouquet at your feet.

Fifth Joyful Mystery - The Finding in the Temple

My God, I give You praise for all circumstances and events of my life, both the good and the challenging. I know that the things that seem troubling to me are really just opportunities for You to teach me and help me to grow. I am thankful for all that You do in my life.

In this you rejoice, although now for a little while you may have to suffer through various trials, so that the genuineness of your faith, more precious than gold that is perishable even though tested by fire, may prove to be for praise, glory, and honor at the revelation of Jesus Christ. ~1 Peter 1:6-7

Fifth Joyful Mystery - Lay the Roses

Mother Mary, I bind these pale blue roses with a petition for the grace of praise through growth and humbly lay this bouquet at your feet.

Day 51

First Sorrowful Mystery - The Agony of Jesus in the Garden

How do I praise God in sorrow? I know, Lord, that is where You are most present - in the pain and suffering, because You took all of that upon Yourself. I praise you, God, in my suffering. I know You are with me.

Why, my soul, are you downcast? Why so disturbed within me? Put your hope in God, for I will yet praise him, my Savior and my God. ~Psalm 42:11

First Sorrowful Mystery - Lay the Roses

Mother Mary, I bind these violet roses with a petition for the grace of praise in suffering and humbly lay this bouquet at your feet.

Second Sorrowful Mystery - Jesus is Scourged at the Pillar

It is hard to see the good when someone suffers. I praise and thank You, Jesus, for Your willingness to take on my pain, to suffer for me.

Finally, brothers and sisters, whatever is true, whatever is noble, whatever is right, whatever is pure, whatever is lovely, whatever is admirable—if anything is excellent or praiseworthy—think about such things. ~Philippians 4:8

Second Sorrowful Mystery - Lay the Roses

Mother Mary, I bind these violet roses with a petition for the grace of compassion and humbly lay this bouquet at your feet.

Third Sorrowful Mystery - Jesus is Crowned with Thorns

I praise You, Jesus, as my Lord and King. I know who You are and what You want to be in my life. I worship You properly above all things.

Let us come before him with thanksgiving and extol him with music and song. For the Lord is the great God, the great King above all gods. ~Psalm 95:2-3

Third Sorrowful Mystery - Lay the Roses

Mother Mary, I bind these violet roses with a petition for the grace of putting God first and humbly lay this bouquet at your feet.

Fourth Sorrowful Mystery - Jesus Carries His Cross

I give You praise, Lord, for Your acceptance of the cross for me. I thank You and celebrate my own cross that allows me to be more conformed to You.

Blessed be the Lord, who daily bears us up; God is our salvation. ~Psalm 68:19

Fourth Sorrowful Mystery - Lay the Roses

Mother Mary, I bind these violet roses with a petition for the grace of connection with God and humbly lay this bouquet at your feet.

Fifth Sorrowful Mystery - The Crucifixion and Death of our Lord Jesus Christ

Lord Jesus Christ, I give You praise and honor as You hang upon the cross. This is Your throne where You show Your true power and glory. I worship You as I should.

It is written: 'As surely as I live,' says the Lord, 'every knee will bow before me; every tongue will acknowledge God.' ~Romans 14:11

Fifth Sorrowful Mystery - Lay the Roses

Mother Mary, I bind these violet roses with a petition for the grace of true worship of God and humbly lay this bouquet at your feet.

Day 52

First Glorious Mystery - The Resurrection of Jesus

To You be glory, Jesus. When I am in doubt and despair, You appear to me alive and risen from the dead to restore my relationship with You. I give You praise!

Where, O death, is your victory? Where, O death, is your sting? But thanks be to God who gives us the victory through our Lord Jesus Christ. ~1 Corinthians 15:55,57

First Glorious Mystery - Lay the Roses

Mother Mary, I bind these pure white roses with a petition for the grace of restoration and humbly lay this bouquet at your feet.

Second Glorious Mystery - The Ascension of Jesus into Heaven

Jesus, how can I not be filled with joy and a desire to worship You? You have given everything for me and have set a light on the path for me to follow. I thank You!

Through Jesus, therefore, let us continually offer to God a sacrifice of praise, the fruit of lips that openly profess his name. And do not forget to do good and to share with others, for with such sacrifices God is pleased. ~Hebrews 13:15-16

Second Glorious Mystery - Lay the Roses

Mother Mary, I bind these pure white roses with a petition for the grace of joyful worship and humbly lay this bouquet at your feet.

Third Glorious Mystery - The Descent of the Holy Spirit

I praise You, Holy Spirit, for my encounter with You. Your grace and presence will be with me always. I honor You!

Therefore, we who are receiving the unshakable kingdom should have gratitude, with which we should offer worship pleasing to God in reverence and awe. For our God is a consuming fire. ~Hebrews 12:28-29

Third Glorious Mystery - Lay the Roses

Mother Mary, I bind these pure white roses with a petition for the grace of unity with God and humbly lay this bouquet at your feet.

Fourth Glorious Mystery - The Assumption of Mary into Heaven

All that Mary did was to praise God. I join her in my adoration of You, Lord, as I celebrate her entrance into heaven.

LORD, God of hosts, who is like you? Mighty LORD, your faithfulness surrounds you. ~Psalm 89:9

Fourth Glorious Mystery - Lay the Roses

Mother Mary, I bind these pure white roses with a petition for the grace of reverence of God and humbly lay this bouquet at your feet.

Fifth Glorious Mystery - The Coronation of Mary as Queen of Heaven and Earth

What a glorious sight as the lowly handmaid is honored as Queen. I join her in proclaiming Your greatness, O Lord my God.

Praise be to the God and Father of our Lord Jesus Christ, who has blessed us in the heavenly realms with every spiritual blessing in Christ. ~Ephesians 1:3

Fifth Glorious Mystery - Lay the Roses

Mother Mary, I bind these pure white roses with a petition for the grace of praise and humbly lay this bouquet at your feet.

Day 53

First Luminous Mystery - The Baptism of Jesus

I praise You, God. I thank You for my baptism and for the baptism of all those who came before me that led to mine and brought me into the faith. I thank You, Jesus, for sanctifying the waters of baptism for me. I will live my baptismal vows well. It is my faith, the faith of the Church. If I am a godparent, I will help my godchild and support them on their faith journey.

Let everything that has breath praise the Lord! Praise the Lord! ~Psalm 150:6

First Luminous Mystery - Lay the Roses

Mother Mary, I bind these orange roses with a petition for the grace of commitment to Christ and humbly lay this bouquet at your feet.

Second Luminous Mystery - The Wedding at Cana

God, I praise You for the miracles that You work, both the large public miracles and the small ones that are behind the scenes. I know that I can pray for miracles and believe that You do perform them. I will cooperate with Your plans to work miracles in my life and in the lives of others. I let You use me in the process of these marvels. I will help others to greater faith by my cooperation with You. I will live in the glory of the miracles You have already given me, and I will share them with others.

He is your praise; he is your God, who has done for you those great and awesome things that your own eyes have seen. ~Deuteronomy 10:21

Second Luminous Mystery - Lay the Roses

Mother Mary, I bind these orange roses with a petition for the grace of belief in the miraculous and humbly lay this bouquet at your feet.

Third Luminous Mystery - The Proclamation of the Kingdom of God

I praise You, Jesus, and thank You for ushering in the kingdom of God. You are the fulfillment. I will do my part in helping to bring about that kingdom. I will pray for it and for God's will to be done in all things. I surrender to God's will in all things. I will pray for myself and others and will accompany others when I am called to. Lord, I will help You in their healing and conversion. I profess my belief in You, my God, and will live my faith.

Yours, Lord, is the greatness and the power and the glory and the majesty and the splendor, for everything in heaven and earth is yours. Yours, Lord, is the kingdom; you are exalted as head over all. ~1 Chronicles 29:11

Third Luminous Mystery - Lay the Roses

Mother Mary, I bind these orange roses with a petition for the grace of living faith and humbly lay this bouquet at your feet.

Fourth Luminous Mystery - The Transfiguration of Jesus

I praise You and I glorify You, Lord. I recognize Your divinity and I bask in Your Light. I choose the better part at Your feet, being filled with Your Light so I can share it with others. I will work with those whom You have placed with me on the journey. Together we will let You enlighten us and then together we take Your Light to the world.

His glory covered the heavens, and his praise filled the earth; his splendor spread like the light. ~Habakkuk 3:3-4

Fourth Luminous Glorious - Lay the Roses

Mother Mary, I bind these orange roses with a petition for the grace of cooperation and humbly lay this bouquet at your feet.

Fifth Luminous Mystery - The Institution of the Eucharist

God, I praise You. I thank You for all You give me, especially for the Church with all its blessings. I thank You for the sacraments that give me grace and for the priesthood which represents You. I am eternally grateful for the Eucharist, which is You, Jesus. I recognize You for who You are. I receive You, being open to all You have for me. I go out on mission to give that grace to the world.

I am the living bread that came down from heaven; whoever eats this bread will live forever; and the bread that I will give is my flesh for the life of the world." ~John 6:51

Fifth Luminous Mystery - Lay the Roses

Mother Mary, I bind these orange roses with a petition for the grace of anointed mission and humbly lay this bouquet at your feet.

Day 54

First Sorrowful Mystery - The Agony of Jesus in the Garden

I praise You God through pain. I give You glory in the agony, even when I do not feel like it. That is where true strength is found. I may not know how You are working in my sorrows and anxieties, but I know that You can bring good out of all things. I trust in that.

Martha and Mary trusted in Your ability and sent for You when Lazarus was ill. I reach out to You too when I am in need.

Greater love has no one than this: to lay down one's life for one's friends. ~John 15:13

First Sorrowful Mystery - Lay the Roses

Mother Mary, I bind these blood red roses with a petition for the grace of trust and humbly lay this bouquet at your feet.

Second Sorrowful Mystery - Jesus is Scourged at the Pillar

I live my life from now on in the knowledge of Your love for me that took on my sin. I repent when needed. I vow to amend my life where necessary. I accept the healing You wish to give me.

Just as Martha accepted Your redirection, so do I. May my whole life give You glory.

It was our pain that he bore, our sufferings he endured. We thought of him as stricken, struck down by God and afflicted, but he was pierced for our sins, crushed for our iniquity. He bore the punishment that makes us whole, by his wounds we were healed. ~Isaiah 53:4-5

Second Sorrowful Mystery - Lay the Roses

Mother Mary, I bind these blood red roses with a petition for the grace of a firm purpose of amendment and humbly lay this bouquet at your feet.

Third Sorrowful Mystery - Jesus is Crowned with Thorns

Jesus, I recognize You as the true King. I put You first in my life. I try to help others see that You are King by how I live, by what I say and do.

Lazarus knew firsthand of Your kingship, having been brought to life again by You. I join him in honoring You the way I should. Martha came to believe in You as her Lord. Mary did too as she desired to sit at Your feet. Help me to live with You as my King.

Let the heavens be glad and the earth rejoice; let them say among the nations: The LORD is king. ~1 Chronicles 16:31

Third Sorrowful Mystery - Lay the Roses

Mother Mary, I bind these blood red roses with a petition for the grace of faith in action and humbly lay this bouquet at your feet.

Fourth Sorrowful Mystery - Jesus Carries His Cross

You tell me that Your burden is light, and Your yoke is easy. I want always to be yoked with You, Jesus. I know that it is easy when I carry my cross for love of You and love of others as You did. May we always be together. With You I can do all things.

You lovingly let Martha know when she was anxious and worried. I give my burdens to You, Lord. I praise You in my struggle.

"Come to me, all you who labor and are burdened, and I will give you rest. Take my yoke upon you and learn from me, for I am meek and humble of heart; and you will find rest for yourselves. For my yoke is easy, and my burden light." ~Matthew 11:28-30

Fourth Sorrowful Mystery - Lay the Roses

Mother Mary, I bind these blood red roses with a petition for the grace of unity with Christ and humbly lay this bouquet at your feet.

Fifth Sorrowful Mystery - The Crucifixion and Death of our Lord Jesus Christ

Jesus, I thank You for the great gift of love and strength through Your death. I accept Your help to show this type of love to all others. Lazarus knew what it was like to experience death and also to be brought back to new life by You. I have died with You in baptism. I allow You to bring me to new life.

And just as Moses lifted up the serpent in the desert, so must the Son of Man be lifted up, so that everyone who believes in him may have eternal life. ~John 3:14-15

Fifth Sorrowful Mystery - Lay the Roses

Mother Mary, I bind these blood red roses with a petition for the grace of love of others and humbly lay this bouquet at your feet.

In Conclusion

Thank you so much for praying this novena with me! I hope that you continue to pray the rosary. It is a beautiful and powerfully effective prayer.

If praying the rosary like this was new to you, I encourage you to let the Holy Spirit guide you in your prayer. Place yourself in the mystery in a quiet, contemplative way, as Mary would, reflecting in your heart. Then ask the Holy Spirit to direct you. I often say, "God, what do You want me to see?" Notice what catches your attention and focus on that. It may be an object. Look at it more closely. Observe the details. It might be an idea, such as peace or light. Continue to ask God what you need to see and hear. Or you can ask Mary or Saint Joseph or someone in the mystery to take you by the hand and lead you.

Be patient. If you aren't used to praying in this way, it may take practice. Go into the meditation with no expectation. Let the Lord guide you where you need to go.

I want to share one last thing. Below is a poem I wrote about the rosary. It was written with the order of the rosary in mind, as it goes through each part.

Thank you again for all of the blessings that were brought about by your prayers. I hope you have a greater love for the rosary and will experience it in a new way. God wants you to grow closer to Him. Always remember that He loves you very deeply and is always with you!

Strand of Roses

I grasp my cord on which the rose buds wait
willing to be given life
by my breath, His breath, hers

Each one blossoming
opening to reveal the love inside
The hidden mystery unveiling itself
little by little

The needs are many
to be lifted up
holding on to hope
in my heart yet for me to give away
Let them fly to the clouds
heaven awaits

The sign is given
All things done for You, with You, in You
You in me
All that I am is from You
All that I have is by You
may You be all that is in me

My profession
belief from Your Heart to mine
mine to yours

All that You say
I say too
All has come to pass
all is in being
You forever, eternity

What you have taught, I give back
perfection from You
praise, obedience, care, mercy, healing, protection
All

Virtues sought
practiced, rediscovered
with her help

Worship that is due
all praise forever

The walk begins
continues really
for it is always in motion
Being led along the path
deeper into the Hearts
awakening, understanding

I release my roses, strewn about
their fragrance pervades the air
their light reveals the way
they keep me on the journey that is mine

Each petal a new insight
illumination and connection
taking me deeper, closer

Opening my eyes to see with Yours
The reality that has always been there
just out of reach
You allow me to grasp

Our worlds uniting
but mine has always been Yours
Now I give it freely
as You freely give to me

Roses swirl around me
being swept up
Caught into the bouquet
that I offer now to you
but is always mine as well

In Gratitude

I want to thank those who have greatly helped to make this book possible. My dear friends Sue Busse and Lyn Mettler worked to put this book together. Sue was instrumental in the actual process of it. I did very little except write and edit. She even made the first copies of the book by hand!

Lyn assisted with some of the writing in the introduction and the editing and also just helped to figure things out.

I have several good friends who contributed the lovely artwork for this book. Jessica Bohrer, Emily Meiner, and Israel Perez all offered their original art. I feel this really makes Our Blessed Mother's Crown of Roses come to life for us.

And I also want to thank the many friends who prayed this novena with me. They also prayed for me and offered feedback and encouragement to make this happen. Prayer is truly powerful. My goal in making this book is to encourage more prayer and hopefully more meaningful and contemplative prayer to lead to a deeper relationship with our Lord.

Art Credits:
Jessica Bohrer: pages 8, 9, 27, 76, 95, 160, footers, spine
Emily Meiner: pages 4, 49, 115, 179, 182, front cover, back
Israel Perez: title page, page 136

Reflections on A Crown of Roses

"I want to share that I have never really developed a love of the rosary. There have been periods where I have prayed it regularly, but it was for myself. So that I could check off the box. Since the Holy Spirit made me say yes to your question (to join the rosary novena), I have truly wanted to pray and looked for times each day to do so. I am looking forward to today's rosary in a way I never have before now.
From my heart, thank you for taking on this ministry." ~Kathy K.

"I truly could not have made it these last 54 days without being drawn closer to Jesus and Mary. As always, I have felt loved and cared for -with this time with them, but the beautiful reflections that you so lovingly shared with us were exactly what I needed to help me each day...to calm my soul as I prayed."~ Patricia S.

"Oh, how I loved this novena!! My favorite part of every day was praying this each morning. This novena took me deeper into the mysteries like never before, and I experienced a true intimacy with both Mary and Jesus."
~Dawn H.

"I just perused the new book. What a beautiful tribute to our Mother. Thank you! I will enjoy praying the Novena with our community through this inspiring devotional." ~Ted H.

"Thank you. These are beautiful meditations. I can't fully explain how I have changed in my prayer life. How much closer I feel to Mary and how much closer she has led me to Jesus. It has really been a privilege to pray this rosary."~ Loretta F.

"I just want to thank you for sharing your Rosary Novena. I loved it! I get so used to saying the prayers of the Rosary 'by rote' and this really helped

me focus on the prayers and mysteries. You truly have a gift; thank you for sharing it!"~ Eve G.

"I have found this experiencing the rosary with so many others extremely spiritually enriching. Your reflections are so beautiful and come from a heart filled with love of God and the Blessed Mother. You are truly inspired and guided by the Holy Spirit."~ Carol A.

"I've tried before to pray a 54-day novena but had failed to follow through. Praying with your elegant and engaging book, it felt as if I was doing so as part of a local community. Because of this, each day I prioritized time to reflect and then pray the rosary. Eventually, with the help of some of the reflections, I learned to slow down and truly breathe while praying. Thank you! As you say, the skillful illustrations bring A Crown of Roses to life." ~Jimmy S.